Taking
Refuge
in
Buddhism

Taking Refuge in
Buddhism

by Sujin Boriharnwanaket

Translated from
the original Thai by
Nina van Gorkom

First Edition
April
2000

zolag • London

First Edition
April 2000
zolag
46 Fircroft Road
Tooting Bec
London
SW17 7PS
Find us on the web at
www.zolag.co.uk

ISBN 1 897633 20 3

British Library Cataloguing in Publication Data.
*A CIP record for this book is available from the
British Library.*

Printed in Great Britain by:
Biddles Ltd., Guildford, and King's Lynn.

Front cover picture:
Battersea Park Peace Pagoda, London.

Contents

From the sponsor:

Dedicated to the memory of
John Kirkpatrick (1921-1999)

Preface

This book is a compilation of Discussions on Buddhism Ms Sujin had with Cambodians in 1992 and 1993, in Cambodia and in Nakorn Nāyok, near the border between Thailand and Cambodia. The teacher of the group of Cambodians, Mr Buth Sawong, had learnt Thai in seven years in order to follow Ms Sujin's radio program on Buddhism which can be heard also in Cambodia. Several years ago a blind friend had encouraged him to listen to Ms Sujin. During the day Mr Buth Sawong studied Buddhism and in the evening he explained to others what he had learnt about the development of right understanding of mental phenomena and physical phenomena in daily life. People generally thought that they had to sit and be tranquil in order to develop wisdom as taught by the Buddha; what they learnt from Ms Sujin about the development of understanding in their daily lives was quite new to them. When I met Mr Buth Sawong in Thailand he said that he had never heard before such teaching of the development of right understanding. He was very happy to learn that this development was to be done in daily life. The Thais helped Mr Buth Sawong with a new radio station and now he has his own program on two different stations. He also translated my "Abhidhamma in Daily Life" into Cambodian.

One of the members of his group is a magician famous all over Cambodia. He also entertained us with magic tricks when he was in Thailand. More extraordinary is that he, after each magic show, gives a lecture on Buddhism, explaining that his tricks are an illusion and that illusion is different from reality. He said that people should not only have enjoyment in what is only an illusion, but that they should also learn more about realities in their daily lives.

This is the Middle Way the Buddha taught. People do not have to force themselves to follow difficult ascetic practices, they can develop understanding of the phenomena which naturally appear in their daily lives, including defilements.

The Buddha taught the development of right understanding of all that is real, of all the phenomena of our life as they appear through the five senses and the mind. This understanding can eventually lead to the eradication of all faults and vices. The development of insight or right understanding was the subject of the discussions on Buddhism held in Cambodia. Ms Sujin stressed time and again that the conditions for the growth of understanding are above all listening to the Dhamma and considering what one has heard. By listening and considering, the right conditions are accumulated for the arising of direct awareness of realities and at such moments direct understanding of them can be developed. The Buddha taught that there is no person, no being, no self. What we take for our mind and our body are only different mental phenomena and physical phenomena which arise because of conditions and then fall away. All realities and thus also mindfulness and understanding are non-self. There is nobody who can control the arising of awareness and understanding; there is no particular method which has to be followed for the development of right understanding. Theoretical understanding of realities acquired by listening and considering is the foundation for direct understanding of them.

This book consists of questions and answers. At each meeting there was an interpreter who translated Ms Sujin's words into Cambodian and also summarized the questions of the listeners. In chapter 6 we read about Ms Sujin's personal life and about the way she started to be interested in the Buddhist teachings. She mentions the lack of Thai translations of the scriptures and commentaries before 1957. When there were more translations available she used more quotations from the scriptures during her lectures and thereby greatly encouraged people to read the scriptures themselves. In this way they would be guided by the teachings themselves and not follow blindly other people. Moreover, Ms Sujin has done a great deal to promote the translations of the old commentaries to the Suttas into Thai. In the Thai editions of the Suttas today each sutta is followed by its commentary.

I hope the reader will be inspired when reading about the development of right understanding in daily life, just as our Cambodian friends were inspired. Mr Buth Sawong showed his great confidence and deep respect to Ms Sujin's guidance, because he considered her as a mother, as someone who gave him a new life. If one learns to apply the Buddha's teachings it is true that a new life begins. With my deepest appreciation of Ms Sujin's guidance and with great pleasure I offer the translation of this book on the development of right understanding to the English readers. I also wish to acknowledge my appreciation to the "Dhamma Study and Propagation Foundation"; to the sponsor of the printing of this edition, Robert Kirkpatrick: and to the publisher Alan Weller who have made possible the publication of this book.

The quotations in English from the Suttas are mostly taken from the texts of the Pali Text Society (73 Lime Walk, Headington, Oxford, OX 37 AD, England).

I have added footnotes to the text in order to make the reading of this book easier. I shall now in my Introduction give an explanation and summary of some notions and terms of the Buddhist teachings in order to help those who may not be familiar with them.

Introduction

For the development of understanding of the phenomena of our life in ourselves and around ourselves, it is essential to know the difference between what is real in the conventional sense and what is real in the absolute or ultimate sense. Before we learnt about the Buddhist teachings we only knew conventional realities such as person, world, animal or tree. The Buddha taught about absolute or ultimate realities, in Pāli paramattha dhammas. Ultimate realities or as they often are referred to in this book, dhammas, have each their own characteristic, their own function, and they are true for everybody. We are used to thinking of mind and body, but what we take for mind are in reality different moments of consciousness, cittas, which change all the time. Citta is a mental phenomenon or nāma, it experiences an object. What we take for body are different physical phenomena, rūpas, which arise and fall away. Rūpa does not experience anything. Nāma and rūpa are absolute realities, each with their own unalterable characteristic. Seeing, for example, is nāma, it experiences visible object. It has its own characteristic which cannot be changed: seeing is always seeing, for everybody, no matter how we name it. The names of realities can be changed but their characteristics are unalterable. After having seen visible object we think of the shape and form of a person or a thing, but that is not seeing, it is thinking of a concept which is real in conventional sense, not in the absolute sense. In our life there are cittas which are seeing, hearing, smelling, tasting, or experiencing tangible object and there are also cittas which on account of such experiences think of concepts. This is our daily life and through the Buddha's teachings we will be less deluded about our life. We will learn what is real in the absolute sense and what is only a conventional reality or concept.

There is only one citta at a time which arises and falls away, to be succeeded by the next citta. Each citta experiences an object. Seeing is a citta experiencing visible object through the eyesense, hearing is another type of citta experiencing sound through the earsense. Different cittas experience objects through the six doorways, namely, through the five senses and the mind. Cittas are variegated: some cittas are wholesome, kusala, some are unwholesome, akusala, and some are neither kusala nor akusala. There is one citta arising at a time, but each citta is accompanied by several mental factors, cetasikas, which each perform their own function while they assist the citta in knowing the object. Some cetasikas such as feeling or remembrance, saññā, accompany each citta, whereas other types of cetasikas accompany only particular types of citta. Attachment, lobha, aversion, dosa, and ignorance, moha, are akusala cetasikas which accompany only akusala cittas. Non-attachment, alobha, non-aversion, adosa, and wisdom, amoha or paññā, are sobhana cetasikas, beautiful cetasikas, which can accompany only sobhana cittas.

Citta and cetasika, which are both mental phenomena, nāma, arise because of their appropriate conditions. Wholesome qualities and unwholesome qualities which arose in the past can condition the arising of such qualities at present. Since our life is an unbroken series of cittas, succeeding one another, wholesome qualities and unwholesome qualities can be accumulated from one moment to the next moment, and thus there are conditions for their arising at the present time.

Some cittas are results of akusala kamma and kusala kamma, they are vipākacittas. Kamma is intention or volition. When there is unwholesome volition it can motivate an unwholesome deed which can bring an unpleasant result later on, and when there is wholesome volition it can motivate a wholesome deed which can bring a pleasant result later on.

Akusala kamma and kusala kamma are accumulated from one moment of citta to the next moment, and thus they can produce results later on. Kamma produces result in the form of rebirth-consciousness, or, in the course of life, in the form of seeing, hearing, smelling, tasting and the experience of tangible object through the bodysense. These vipākacittas experience pleasant objects or unpleasant objects, depending on the kamma which produces them.

Cittas which experience objects through the six doors arise in a process of cittas. When, for example, hearing arises, it occurs within a series or process of cittas, all of which experience sound. Only hearing-consciousness hears, but the other cittas within that process, which is called the ear-door process, perform each their own function. Hearing-consciousness is vipākacitta, it merely hears the sound, it neither likes it nor dislikes it. After hearing-consciousness has fallen away there are, within that process, akusala cittas or kusala cittas which experience the sound with unwholesomeness or with wholesomeness. There can be akusala cittas with attachment or with aversion towards the sound, or there can be kusala cittas. There are processes of cittas experiencing an object through the eye-door, the ear-door, the nose-door, the tongue-door, the body-door and the mind-door. After the cittas of a sense-door process have fallen away, the object is experienced by cittas arising in a mind-door process, and after that process has been completed there can be other mind-door processes of cittas which think of concepts. Cittas arise and fall away in succession so rapidly that it seems that cittas such as seeing and thinking of what is seen occur at the same time, but in reality there are different types of citta arising in different processes. We believe, for example, that we see a table, but in reality there is a process of cittas experiencing visible object through the eyesense, and then there is a process of cittas experiencing visible object through the mind-door, and later on there are other mind-door processes of cittas which think of the concept of table. For the development of right understanding it is important to know that there are different cittas which experience different objects through the six doorways.

Citta and cetasika are mental phenomena, in Pāli: nāma. Nāma experiences an object whereas physical phenomena, in Pāli: rūpa, do not know or experience anything. What we call the body consists of different kinds of rūpa which arise and then fall away. Rūpas arise and fall away in groups or units of rūpas. Each group consists of several kinds of rūpas which always include four kinds of rūpas which are called the four Great Elements, as explained in Chapter 1. Rūpas of the body are conditioned by four factors, namely, by kamma, citta, temperature and nutrition. Rūpas outside, such as rūpas of a table or a tree, are conditioned only by temperature.

The Buddha explained in detail about the different nāmas and rūpas of our life and the conditions through which they arise. Theoretical understanding of nāma and rūpa is a foundation for direct understanding of them, and this can be developed by sati, awareness or mindfulness of the nāma and rūpa appearing at the present moment. There are many levels of sati; sati is heedful, non-forgetful, of what is wholesome. There is sati with generosity, dāna, with the observance of moral conduct, sīla, with the development of tranquil meditation, samatha, and with the development of insight or right understanding, vipassanā. In the development of insight, sati is mindful of whatever reality presents itself through one of the six doors. Absolute realities, nāma and rūpa, not concepts, are the objects of mindfulness and right understanding.

Paññā develops progressively in different stages of insight knowledge. When the first stage of insight knowledge arises there is no doubt about the difference between the characteristic of nāma and the characteristic of rūpa. At a higher stage of insight the arising and falling away of nāma and rūpa, their impermanence, can be penetrated. In the course of the development of insight a clearer understanding is gained of the three characteristics of conditioned realities, namely the characteristics of impermanence, dukkha and non-self.

Dukkha is translated as suffering or unsatisfactoriness. It is the unsatisfactoriness due to the impermanence of conditioned realities, as Ms Sujin explains in Chapter 5. When paññā has been developed to the degree that enlightenment can be attained, the four noble Truths are penetrated, which are: dukkha, the origination of dukkha, the cessation of dukkha and the Path leading to the cessation of dukkha. The origination of dukkha is craving. The Buddha explained that so long as there is craving there will be dukkha. There will be the arising and falling away of nāma and rūpa again and again and this is dukkha. When the last citta of this life, the dying-consciousness, has fallen away, it will be succeeded by the first citta of the next life, the rebirth-consciousness. At rebirth there is again arising and falling away of nāma and rūpa, and this is dukkha. Ignorance and craving are the conditions for the continuation in the cycle of birth and death, and so long as we are in this cycle there is dukkha. When wisdom has been fully developed all defilements are eradicated and this means the end of rebirth, the end of dukkha.

Defilements are progressively eradicated at the four stages of enlightenment: the stage of the streamwinner, sotāpanna, the stage of the once-returner, sakadāgāmī, the stage of the non-returner, anāgāmī, and the stage of the arahat, the perfected one. The arahat who has eradicated all defilements, will not be reborn when he has passed away.

The third noble Truth, the cessation of dukkha, is nibbāna. At the attainment of enlightenment nibbāna, the unconditioned reality, is experienced. Citta, cetasika and rūpa are conditioned realities which arise and fall away, they are dukkha. Nibbāna is the ultimate reality which is unconditioned, it does not arise and fall away, it is not dukkha. Nibbāna is the end of the unsatisfactoriness inherent in all conditioned realities which arise and fall away.

The fourth noble Truth is the Way leading to the cessation of dukkha, and this is the eightfold Path. We come across the terms the development of the eightfold Path, the development of insight, vipassanā, and the development of satipaṭṭhāna or the four Applications of Mindfulness. All these terms pertain to the development of right understanding of mental phenomena, nāma, and physical phenomena, rūpa. By the teaching of the four Applications of Mindfulness the Buddha showed that all nāmas and rūpas which appear naturally in our daily life can be the objects of mindfulness and right understanding.

Chapter 1

Mental Phenomena and Physical Phenomena
Discussion in Battambang (Part One)

Sujin: You had questions about "Mindfulness of the Body" which is one of the four "Applications of Mindfulness". There is no doubt about it that we all have a body, but we used to take it for "mine" or "self" before we listened to the Dhamma. After having studied the Dhamma we learnt that all realities, all "dhammas"[1], are non-self, anattā. We should have right understanding of the term "dhamma", a reality which is non-self.

The Buddha did not only teach the "Four Applications of Mindfulness", mahā-satipaṭṭhāna, he taught all that is contained in the "Tipiṭaka". His teachings have come to us today in the "Tipiṭaka": the three "Collections" of the Vinaya or the Book of Discipline for the monks, the Suttanta or Discourses, and the Abhidhamma or "Higher Teachings". All the different parts of the Tipiṭaka are in conformity with each other because they contain the truth which the Buddha himself penetrated at the attainment of Buddhahood when he was seated under the Bodhi-tree.

When we have listened to the Dhamma, even though we have not heard all of it, and when we have acquired profound understanding of the meaning and of the characteristics of the realities the Buddha taught, we will be convinced that the three "Collections" have to be in conformity with each other.

[1] The word "dhamma" has several meanings. It can mean the Buddha's teaching, but in a wider sense dhamma is everything that is real. Citta, cetasika and rūpa are dhammas, realities, which each have their own characteristic.

The Tipiṭaka explains all conditioned realities as citta, consciousness, cetasika, mental factors accompanying citta, and rūpa, physical phenomena. Thus, if there would not be citta, cetasika and rūpa, there would be no Tipiṭaka. The Tipiṭaka teaches us that the realities the Buddha penetrated at his attainment of Buddhahood are non-self. When we speak about the body we have to understand what the body, which is devoid of self, really is. Besides, the body does not arise alone, without citta and cetasikas. When there is understanding, paññā, it knows the truth of realities. It does not only understand the characteristics of the realities we call the "body", but it also knows the different characteristics of the mental realities, of citta and cetasikas, which appear. Paññā can realize that what we used to take for "mine" or "I", or for the world, are only different types of " dhammas", realities, namely: citta, cetasika and rūpa. It is most beneficial to study the Dhamma. When we study the teachings we should also verify ourselves the truth of what we learnt, we should investigate ourselves the realities which appear in our daily life. In that way we will acquire a deeper understanding of them. For this reason, I would like the listeners to consider the Dhamma and to try to answer their questions themselves. You have questions about "Mindfulness of the Body", but when you investigate the truth yourselves, you will see more clearly that there are, besides the body, also citta and cetasika.

Buth Sawong: Some people would like to know the meaning of "seeing the body in the body", as is stated in the "Satipaṭṭhāna Sutta" in the section on "Mindfulness of the Body".

Sujin: We could discuss about many realities, but since the time is limited for this Dhamma discussion I would like first of all to go into an important point, namely, the meaning of "dhamma". Everything which is real is dhamma. The body is dhamma. When we touch the body, softness or hardness appears. Softness and hardness are characteristics of realities, they are elements which each have their own unchangeable characteristic. Softness is always softness and hardness is always hardness, no matter whether we touch the body or things outside. When paññā understands that the characteristic of softness or of hardness, no matter whether it appears in the body or outside the body, is in each case the same reality, the same element, paññā can develop. When paññā has become keener it can realize that these elements arise because of conditions and then fall away completely. In this way there can be detachment from the conception that these elements are "self". Then one sees "the body in the body", which means that one understands that the body is not me, mine or self.

Buth Sawong: What we call "the body", kāya, is made up of different elements which are joined together. Of what does the body consist?

Sujin: What we call "the body" is made up of different realities. Because of the joining together of different elements we can say that we have eyes, ears, nose, tongue and body, or we can distinguish different parts of the body, such as hair of the head, hair of the body, nails, teeth, skin, etc.

Buth Sawong: When I hear the sentence, "seeing the body in the body", I do not understand to what refers the second word "body" of this sentence.

Sujin: People are inclined to attach too much importance to terms, such as, "seeing the body in the body". They wonder which body they have to see, or how they have to see the body in the body. People know that they have eyes, ears, nose, tongue and body, but when and in what way do these appear? They should know that there is the characteristic of hardness in the whole body, from head to toes. Wherever we touch the body, hardness or softness appears right at that spot. There is at that moment impingement of an object on the rūpa which is bodysense[2]. The bodysense is a necessary condition for the experience of tangible object. If there were no bodysense the characteristics of hardness and softness could not be experienced.

The realities which appear through the six doors, the doors of the senses and the mind, can be seen as six distinct worlds, each different from the other: the world appearing through the eyes, the ears, the nose, the tongue, the body and the mind. This is called in the scriptures, "the world in the discipline of the ariyan"[3]. This helps us to understand that rūpas of the body can only be experienced right at the spot where there is touching, just for a moment, and that only one characteristic of rūpa at a time can appear. The whole body cannot be directly experienced. A rūpa which has arisen impinges, it appears and then it falls away immediately.

This is the meaning of "seeing the body in the body". We should not think of the terms "body in the body" and wonder what the meaning is of the first word "body" and what of the second one. It is important to understand that there are different moments of experience: the moment of seeing is different from the moment of hearing. Seeing, hearing, smelling, tasting and the experience of hardness which impinges on the bodysense are all different moments of citta. At this moment there is the impingement of hardness on the bodysense. So long as there is still "attā-saññā", the wrong remembrance of self[4], one takes everything for

[2] The rūpa which is bodysense is all over the the body. It is capable of receiving tangible object which impinges on it, such as the rūpas which are hardness, softness, heat, cold, motion or pressure.

[3] Ariyans are those who have realized the truth of realities and attained enlightenment. We read about the world in the ariyan discipline in the Kindred Sayings IV, Kindred Sayings on Sense, Second Fifty, Ch 4, § 84, Transitory.

[4] Attā means self and saññā is the cetasika, mental factor arising with the citta, which is remembrance. Saññā arises with each citta and it

"mine" or "self"; one believes, for example, that "my finger" touches a certain "thing" which is hard. However, if we have understood that there is no self, only dhammas, realities, and if there can be awareness of hardness which appears because of impingement on the bodysense, we will see that the rūpa which is hardness is a reality which has arisen because of conditions. If the rūpa which is hardness has not arisen it cannot appear. The hardness which has arisen and appears must fall away again. Hardness is not "self" or "mine", there is no self who can exert control over it.

Buth Sawong: I understand that we have eyes, that there are things which appear through eyesense and that there is a reality which experiences what appears through eyesense. Is this what is called, "seeing the body in the body"?

Sujin: At such a moment there is not the "Application of Mindfulness of the Body", seeing the body in the body. We should remember that there are four "Applications of Mindfulness" or satipaṭṭhāna: mindfulness of the body, of feeling, of citta and of dhammas. All that is included in the four "Applications of Mindfulness", the objects of mindfulness, are realities, dhammas. The Buddha taught "Mindfulness of the Body" because, from birth to death, from life to life, we cling to the whole body, from head to toes, taking it for "my body", for self. When there is "mindfulness of the body", sati is aware of the realities we are used to taking for "my body". When the characteristics of the "four Great Elements" (mahā-bhūta rūpas) [5] are known as they are, there will be detachment from the concept of "my whole body".

remembers or recognizes the object which is experienced. Saññā can be kusala, akusala or neither kusala nor akusala. When saññā is wrong remembrance of self it is akusala, it remembers in a distorted way.

[5] The body is constituted of rūpas which arise in groups or units. Each group consists of several kinds of rūpas and among these are the four "great elements" of solidity, cohesion, heat, and motion.

When we have also studied and thoroughly understood the "Applications of Mindfulness" of feeling, of citta and of dhammas, we will see that the four "Applications of Mindfulness" are in conformity with each other. Realities are classified in many different ways, such as by way of dhātus, elements, khandhas, "aggregates", and āyatanas, bases[6], and these are included in the "Application of Mindfulness of Dhammas". The different classifications of realities show different aspects, but we should remember that everything which is real can be object of mindfulness. The "Application of Mindfulness of the Body" is a separate "application" because everyone clings to the body, taking it for "mine".

Questioner: Citta is the reality which experiences an object. It is said that it "thinks"[7] of an object, because the object is cognized by citta. I would like to know what arises first, the citta or the object. What conditions what?

Sujin: Citta is a difficult subject, it is very detailed. We all have citta; we are seeing, and this is a citta. However, it is necessary to discuss and consider the reality of citta until one has clear understanding of it. Although people at this moment hear about citta, they do not understand what it really is, so long as they have not directly understood the characteristic of citta. Therefore, one needs to listen to the Dhamma again and again.

Citta is the reality which experiences an object. This shows us that citta and the object cannot exist without each other.

---

[6] Conditioned realities can be classified as five khandhas: rūpa-kkhandha, the aggregate of physical phenomena, vedanā-kkhandha, the aggregate of feelings, saññā-kkhandha, the aggregate of remembrance, saṅkhāra-kkhandha, the aggregate of all cetasikas other than feeling and remembrance, and viññāṇa-kkhandha, the aggregate of cittas. There are twelve āyatanas or bases, which are: the sense-organs and the mind-base (cittas), the five objects experienced through the senses and mind-object.

[7] In Pāli there is a word-association between cinteti, thinking, and citta.

It is of no use to speculate about it what arises first and what arises afterwards. The Buddha, at the attainment of Buddhahood, penetrated the truth of all realities. He taught that at the moment of seeing visible object, of hearing sound, of smelling odour, of tasting flavour and of touching tangible object, that in all those cases the rūpa which is sense object arises before the citta which experiences it. The rūpa which arises previously to the citta which experiences it is "prenascence condition" (purejāta paccaya) for that citta[8]. A rūpa which is a sense object impinges on the relevant sense-base, but it is not immediately experienced by citta which is sense-cognition, such as seeing or hearing. When a sense object impinges on a sense-base, there are bhavanga-cittas[9] before a sense-door process of cittas begins and a sense-cognition such as seeing or hearing can arise and experience the object which is impinging[10].

When we consider the relation between seeing-consciousness and visible object which appears through eyes, and the relation between hearing-consciousness and sound which appears through ears, we should remember that the rūpa which is the object of citta must arise previously to the citta which experiences it. Thus, that rūpa conditions the citta by way of "prenascence condition".

There are other kinds of objects besides rūpa, but when we refer to objects which are "prenascence-condition", these are the rūpas which are sense-objects appearing through the five sense-doors. For example, in the case of seeing, the

---

[8] There are many ways realities can be a condition for other realities. Some realities arise at the same time as the realities they condition, others do not.

[9] Bhavanga-cittas or life-continuum arise in between the processes of cittas. These cittas do not experience objects impinging on the sense-doors or the mind-door.

[10] Rūpa lasts longer than citta, thus, it can arise before a sense-door process of cittas begins and be experienced by the cittas arising in that process.

rūpa which is visible object has arisen before the seeing and impinged on the eyesense, and then seeing-consciousness can arise afterwards. When we consider the true nature of nāma and rūpa, they should be distinguished from each other. They each arise because of their own conditions. Rūpa arises and falls away according to its own conditions. There are four factors which can cause the origination of rūpa: kamma, citta, temperature or nutrition[11]. No matter whether citta experiences rūpa or not, rūpa arises and falls away according to its own conditions.

When we discuss the Dhamma we should speak about it in detail. For example, the rūpa which is originated by kamma (kammajā-rūpa) arises all the time from the moment of rebirth-consciousness on. At the moment of birth the rūpa which is produced by kamma arises together with the rebirth-consciousness which is also produced by kamma, and thus, the arising of that rūpa is conditioned by the rebirth-consciousness. After that moment there is time and again, throughout life, the arising of rūpa produced by kamma, but it is not anymore dependant on a citta which arises simultaneously[12], as was the case at rebirth.

There are also rūpas which are originated by citta. These kinds of rūpa are produced by citta at its arising moment. Each moment of citta can be subdivided into three extremely short moments: the arising moment, the moment of its persisting and the moment of its falling away. Each kind of rūpa has a different origin: kamma, citta, temperature or nutrition[13]. A sense object, which is rūpa, experienced by

[11] Rūpas of the body originate from either one of these four factors, but rūpas outside only originate from temperature.

[12] Kamma produces throughout life for example the rūpas which are the sense organs.

[13] As regards rūpa produced by citta, when we are angry we can notice a change in our facial expression. In that case the dosa-mūla-citta produces rūpas. When there is kusala citta with loving kindness our facial expression is different again; it is kusala citta which produces rūpas. As

citta through eyes, ears, nose, tongue, bodysense or mind-door, is originated by one of the four conditioning factors of kamma, citta, temperature or nutrition.

Not only rūpa, but nāma also arises according to its own conditions. For example, each citta which arises and then falls away conditions the arising of the succeeding citta, it is the "contiguity condition" (anantara paccaya) for the following citta. Throughout life there is an uninterrupted series of cittas which succeed one another. The contiguity condition pertains to citta and cetasikas which have fallen away and are the condition for the arising of the succeeding citta and cetasikas. Only nāma can be contiguity condition, rūpa cannot [14]. Nāma and rūpa arise each because of different conditioning factors. Thus, we have to distinguish nāma from rūpa.

---

regards nutrition which produces rūpas, we can sometimes notice that good food or bad food affects the body.

[14] Each citta arises and falls away and is succeeded immediately, without any interval, by the next citta. Rūpas which fall away are not contiguity condition for following rūpas. Rūpas of the body are replaced so long as there are conditions for the production of new rūpas by either one of the four factors of kamma, citta, nutrition or temperature.

Chapter 2

Confidence in the Buddha's Teachings
Discussion in Battambang (Part Two)

Buth Sawong: The listeners have questions about akusala kamma. The citta cannot think of akusala kamma, unwholesome deeds, which have been performed many lives ago. We do not know which akusala kammas we have performed in former lives, but the tendency to akusala has been accumulated, it has become stronger and stronger. What can we do to overcome these accumulated tendencies to akusala?

Sujin: At the attainment of Buddhahood, the Buddha realized the truth of Dhamma by his wisdom which eradicated defilements completely. His teaching is different from all other teachings and methods. The highest degree of wisdom taught by other religions and philosophies is only the degree which can temporarily subdue defilements. Defilements can only be completely eradicated by paññā, wisdom, developed through satipaṭṭhāna, which is actually the development of right understanding of the eightfold Path[15]. Only the Buddha has taught this Path, there is no other way leading to the eradication of defilements.

Bhikkhu: I can develop this Path sometimes, but I want to develop it thoroughly and reach the goal. I do not know how many lives it will take to reach the goal. I have listened to lectures about vipassanā, the development of insight, and I have heard that through insight clinging and the other defilements can be eradicated. The eradication of

---

[15] The development of satipaṭṭhāna or the development of the eightfold Path is the development of right understanding of nāma and rūpa by mindfulness of them when they appear at the present moment.

defilements is most important, but it is extremely difficult, not only for laypeople but also for bhikkhus.

Sujin: The venerable bhikkhu said that the eradication of defilements is difficult, no matter it concerns bhikkhus or laypeople. It is only paññā which can eradicate defilements. If paññā does not arise it is impossible to eradicate them.

Through the accumulation of wisdom together with all the other perfections[16] the Bodhisatta could in his last life, at the attainment of enlightenment, become an omniscient Buddha. Therefore, everyone who is sincerely interested in the Dhamma and who is motivated to study it, should realize that the development of paññā is of the highest benefit. Without paññā it is impossible to eradicate defilements, and if someone who does not develop paññā believes that he can eradicate them, he is utterly deluded. Each person has accumulated many defilements during countless lives, they are accumulated from the past on to this present life, and in this life from the moment of birth until now. However, we should not be discouraged because of this. If we listen to the Dhamma and there is more understanding of it, we can very gradually learn to investigate the characteristics of the realities which appear. This is the way leading to the realization of the truth that dhamma is dhamma, not "I", mine or self.

When someone begins to listen to the Dhamma and sees that the Dhamma is a most difficult subject, he should not become disheartened. If people, instead of being discouraged, begin to develop paññā, they will see that what at first seemed most complicated gradually becomes clearer. The development of right understanding in daily life can become one's habitual inclination and eventually one will be able to fully develop it.

---

[16] The perfections are: generosity, morality, renunciation, wisdom, energy, patience, truthfulness, determination, loving kindness and equanimity.

Buth Sawong: The listeners say that while they are listening to the Dhamma their minds are occupied with the Dhamma, and there is understanding of it. However, when they have finished listening they are distracted, they are absorbed in other things. What should they do in order to cause the citta to be firm and steady with regard to what is wholesome, to be intent on the Dhamma all the time?

Sujin: This is not possible all the time. However, the citta can gradually become more intent on the Dhamma, depending on one's understanding and confidence. The person who has understanding of the Dhamma will not be forgetful of what he has heard, he will ponder over it and consider it. If he has free time he may be inclined to read the scriptures. When he wakes up in the morning he may still think of the Dhamma he has heard. He may, for example, remember what he heard about rūpas of the body. When he touches hardness he can remember that tangible object is not self, not a being, not a person. No matter whether we are asleep or awake, sit, lie down, stand or walk, there is the body; the body is right at hand. There are rūpas of the body appearing whenever we touch what is hard or soft. If someone has firm remembrance of the Dhamma he has heard, and if he has accumulated confidence and the other "spiritual faculties", indriyas [17], there are the right conditions for the arising of mindfulness. Sati can be directly aware of the characteristics of realities which are appearing at the present moment. Then he understands that the dhammas, the realities which are appearing, are not abstract categories. Citta, cetasika and rūpa, all realities which are explained in the Tipiṭaka, are appearing now. The truth of Dhamma pertains to this very moment.

---

[17] These are the wholesome cetasikas of confidence, energy, mindfulness, concentration and wisdom. They are "indriyas"or controlling faculties, they can "control" the defilements which are their opposites.

As paññā develops there can be awareness and investigation of the characteristics of realities and in this way they will be seen more clearly. However, if people cling to paññā it cannot be developed. When we have listened to the Dhamma we acquire more understanding of it, and then, in accordance with what we have learnt about realities, sati can be aware of the characteristics of realities which appear. Some people have a great deal of understanding whereas others do not have much understanding, depending on the extent they have listened to the Dhamma and considered it. Listening to the Dhamma, intellectual understanding of it and pondering over it, these are conditions which support the arising of sati, and in this way the truth about realities can be understood more clearly. However, we should not be negligent with regard to the development of understanding.

We should remember that the Buddha in countless former lives as a Bodhisatta had to accumulate the "perfections". In his last life during which he attained enlightenment, he was a human being, just like all of us who are sitting here. He was seeing visible object through the eyes, hearing sound through the ears and thinking of different things; he was not all the time thinking of the Dhamma. However, he needed to know the true nature of seeing while he was seeing, he needed to know the true nature of hearing while he was hearing. He needed to know these phenomena as they are because they are realities. After seeing and hearing there are like and dislike of what has been seen and heard, and these are also realities which should be known as they are.

The Buddha knew that it is extremely difficult to know the true nature of phenomena such as seeing or hearing, which are realities occurring time and again, in daily life. We could reduce our life to just one moment, because life actually occurs during one moment of citta which experiences an object and is then gone. However, if one is not a Bodhisatta one is absorbed in thinking for a long time about what appears just for a moment through the eyes, the ears, the nose, the tongue, the bodysense or the mind. The Bodhisatta was altogether different from us who are time and again infatuated with what we experience. Since he knew that the way leading to enlightenment was extremely difficult, he accumulated patience, energy and the other perfections, which were necessary conditions to attain Buddhahood. He had endless endurance and he did not become disheartened while he accumulated the perfections with the purpose to penetrate the truth of realities and to be able to teach other beings, so that they also could become free from dukkha just like he himself.

Everybody here has the opportunity to listen to the Dhamma which the Buddha realized at the attainment of enlightenment and which he taught to others as well. You do not need to accumulate the perfections to the extent the Buddha accumulated them for the attainment of Buddhahood, but you can listen to the Dhamma and practise the way the Buddha has shown us.

Listening to the Dhamma, listening intently, is an essential condition for the arising of paññā, there is no other method to develop paññā. If people are listening only superficially they are not really listening to the Dhamma. They may call listening what is not really listening, because what they hear goes in at one ear and out at the other; there is no understanding of what they heard. Listening to the Dhamma is actually paying careful attention to what one hears and pondering over it with understanding. It is most important to remember that listening also means applying what one hears. It is not enough to have only theoretical understanding of what one hears, but one should also practise what the Buddha taught.

Buth Sawong: The venerable bhikkhu says that he has listened already but that he now wants to really practise the Dhamma.

However, he has many different tasks to accomplish with regard to the Order of monks, and because of his work his citta is distracted. He has no opportunity to sit quietly, alone. He has listened to the Dhamma and he has understood what he has heard, but he has no leisure time. He wonders whether there is only one way of practice or more than one, depending on one's way of life. A monk has a way of life which is different from the life of laypeople. He understands that laypeople can practise the Dhamma, but he, as a bhikkhu, has many tasks to do which make it difficult to practise. Since he himself is still young he has a lot of work to do. When he is older he will have more leisure time for the practice.

Sujin: The venerable bhikkhu said that he had listened to the Dhamma already, but, our listening is never enough. Even the arahats in the Buddha's time continued to listen to the Dhamma. The Buddha taught the Dhamma for fortyfive years with the purpose to help people to understand the Truth. We may have listened for a long time, but if we do not come to understand the characteristics of the realities which are appearing, we have not listened long enough yet. It would be better, instead of wanting to practise, to begin to understand the characteristics of the realities appearing at this very moment. We may wish to have no more defilements, but can defilements be eradicated at all if we do not listen to the Dhamma and understand as they are the characteristics of the realities which are appearing?

As regards the venerable bhikkhu's remark about his lack of free time for the practice, not only monks but also laymen have many tasks to fulfil; also many laymen complain that they have no leisure time for the practice. However, the practice of the Dhamma does not depend on the amount of free time one has. Just now, while we are sitting here, there are realities appearing. There are seeing and hearing, and these are real. Also when we are doing our work there

are realities appearing. We cannot select a particular time
for the understanding of this or that reality. It is necessary
to develop paññā which understands the realities which are
appearing in daily life, until there is complete understanding
of them. In this way ignorance, doubt and wrong view of
self can be eradicated.

Buth Sawong: Some listeners ask how to apply the mind so
that they have true confidence in the Buddhist teachings.

Sujin: If people do not understand the Dhamma they cannot
have true confidence in the Buddha's teachings. People may
just repeat the words they have heard about the Buddha,
namely, that he was the most excellent person who eradicated
all defilements completely. However, if they do not
understand what defilements are, where and when they
arise, and how they can be eradicated, they do not know
what real confidence in the fully Enlightened One really
means. Thus, how could confidence arise? When there is
true confidence, there can be the firm conviction that the
Buddha is the Enlightened One, the Perfect One, who has
taught the Dhamma for fortyfive years in order to help all
beings. If someone has firm confidence in the wisdom of
the Buddha, he will be inclined to listen to the Dhamma, to
study it and to ponder over it, he will develop the wisdom
which leads to the realization of the four noble Truths[18]
which the Buddha has taught.

Buth Sawong: Some of the listeners still wonder how to
apply the mind, citta and cetasikas, so that they have firm,
unshakable confidence in the Buddha's teachings.

Sujin: This happens when the lokuttara magga-citta[19] and

---

[18] The Truth of dukkha, the Truth of the origination of dukkha, which is
craving, the Truth of the cessation of dukkha, which is nibbāna, and the
Truth of the Path leading to the cessation of dukkha. Dukkha or suffering
is in this context the unsatisfactoriness due to the impermanence of
conditioned realities.

[19] At the attainment of enlightenment the lokuttara citta, supramundane

the accompanying cetasikas of the sotāpanna, who attains the first stage of enlightenment, arise. Then there is the taking of refuge in the Triple Gem with unshakable confidence due to his realization of the truth of realities. The ordinary person who has not attained enlightenment cannot take refuge in the Triple Gem with unshakable confidence, since he has not yet penetrated the truth of realities. He has not yet realized the truth that the realities appearing at this moment are non-self, that they are arising and falling away, as the Buddha has taught. So long as he has not penetrated the four noble Truths it is still possible for him to change to another belief.

Buth Sawong: I would like to ask once more how to develop the mind, citta and cetasikas, so that there is no longer confusion, no more inclination to change one's belief. At this moment a great variety of beliefs are propagated in Cambodia. I do not want to become confused and drift away from Buddhism, I want to have firm confidence in Buddhism.

Sujin: As I said before, there is the taking of refuge in the Triple Gem with unshakable confidence at the moment the lokuttara citta arises and this is the condition that one will not change anymore to another belief. Before someone can take his refuge in the Triple Gem in such a way, however, he should have confidence in the Buddha's wisdom, and for this confidence he does not only depend on the cetasika saddhā, confidence, but also on other sobhana (beautiful) cetasikas, such as paññā, understanding. If there is just

---

citta, arises which experiences nibbāna. There are four stages of enlightenment and at these stages defilements are progressively eradicated. These stages are: the stage of the sotāpanna or streamwinner, the stage of the sakadāgāmī or once-returner, the stage of the anāgāmī or non-returner, and the stage of the arahat, the perfected one, who has eradicated all defilements. At each stage there is the arising of the magga-citta or path-consciousness which eradicates defilements, and the phala-citta or fruition-consciousness, which is the vipākacitta or result, produced by the magga-citta.

confidence without any understanding, someone's belief in the truth of Buddhism cannot be well-founded.

The Buddhists who feel that they have already confidence in the Buddhist teachings want to pay respect to the Buddha, recite texts and perform their usual tasks as Buddhists. However, they should also listen to the Dhamma and consider what they heard. The more they listen, the more will they understand the wisdom of the Buddha. The Buddha taught the true Dhamma, which everybody can immediately verify, without delay.

Chapter 3

The Meaning of Dhamma
Second Discussion in Battambang

Buth Sawong: How do we have to practise according to the four Applications of Mindfulness?

Sujin: People often ask how they should practise satipaṭṭhāna. Also in Thailand people ask this question. Instead of asking how one should practise and wondering about it, one should, from the beginning, have right understanding of realities, of paramattha dhammas. At this moment we are seeing and hearing; these are realities and, as the Buddha taught, they are non-self. Seeing is just one moment of citta which arises because of conditions and then falls away. One should, instead of wondering how one should practise, understand the realities which appear at this moment. We should understand that seeing is dhamma, hearing is dhamma, thinking is dhamma, smelling is dhamma, tasting is dhamma. Everything is dhamma, dhamma is never lacking. Does paññā know already the characteristics of the dhammas as they are? People should not try to practise in an unnatural way, but they should develop right understanding which knows more and more the characteristics of the realities which are appearing naturally, in daily life.

Buth Sawong: What exactly are dhammas?

Sujin: The word "dhamma" refers to everything which is real. In Pāli the word "sacca-dhamma"[20], true dhamma, is also used, and this word designates that which is real. At this moment there is seeing, and this is real. Therefore, seeing is sacca-dhamma, true dhamma. Hearing is also sacca-

---

[20] sacca means real or true.

dhamma, true dhamma. At this moment there is sacca-
dhamma or dhamma, but when there is ignorance, dhammas
are not known. The Buddha, at the attainment of
enlightenment, penetrated each kind of dhamma, he realized
their true nature. He understood that there are only realities
which arise because of their appropriate conditions and
which are not a being, not a person, not self. However, so
long as we have not understood realities as they are, we
cling to the wrong view of "I am seeing", "I am hearing",
and we cling to the rūpas of the body as "my body".

Buth Sawong: Some people think that our ordinary life at
this moment is not dhamma. Is this correct?

Sujin: If this moment is not dhamma, what is then dhamma?

Buth Sawong: Everything which is seen or heard, no matter
it is alive or not, is dhamma.

Sujin: This is right, and all dhammas are anattā. We read in
the Dhammapada (vs. 277-279, Khuddaka Nikāya):

All conditioned realities are impermanent.
All conditioned realities are dukkha.
All dhammas are anattā[21].

This shows us that everything, nothing excluded, is dhamma,
a reality which is non-self. The characteristic of hardness,
for example, is dhamma. Can anybody cause the arising of
hardness? There isn't anybody who can cause its arising. It
arises because of its appropriate conditions. All phenomena
which are real are dhammas.

Buth Sawong: What is the meaning of the penetration of
the true nature of dhammas?

Sujin: At this moment realities are appearing. Before we are

[21] "All dhammas" include conditioned realities and also the
unconditioned reality, nibbāna.

able to penetrate the true nature of dhammas, we should know, one at a time, the characteristics of realities which we are used to taking for self. The understanding of dhammas is conditioned by listening, studying and considering. In this way we will know that there are two kinds of realities: nāma dhamma, the reality which knows or experiences something, and rūpa dhamma, the reality which does not experience anything. Seeing, for example, is the reality which experiences what appears through the eyes, whereas that which appears through the eyes, visible object, does not know anything. When paññā clearly understands the characteristics of nāma dhamma and rūpa dhamma as only realities which are non-self, it will realize later on their arising and falling away and it will penetrate the four noble Truths.

Buth Sawong: I know that all realities are not self, not a being, not a person. I know that everything with consciousness and without it is impermanent, but I would like to know what the realization of the four noble Truths means. Is knowing that realities are impermanent and dukkha the realization of the four noble Truths?

Sujin: Knowing these things is not yet the penetration of the four noble Truths.

Buth Sawong: Knowing that all realities which are dukkha are non-self, is that right understanding of the truth?

Sujin: Is there understanding of dukkha now, while you are sitting here? What is it that understands dukkha now? In other words, is there at this moment sati, is there the development of the eightfold Path? If sati does not arise, can it be understood that the reality which is seeing is nāma, and that it arises and falls away, that it is impermanent?

Buth Sawong: What are the conditions for the arising of sukha, happiness, and dukkha, suffering?

Sujin: No matter whether a person is Cambodian or Thai,

no matter where he lives, or whether he is rich or poor, so long as he has defilements he will have dukkha. Because of lobha, attachment, dosa, aversion, and moha, ignorance, he is worried and oppressed, and thus he is bound to suffer. There isn't anybody who is really happy and peaceful unless he has become an arahat who has eradicated all defilements and who, when he passes away, attains final nibbāna. The arahat will not be reborn and thus there will not be anymore dukkha for him.

I appreciate very much the interest in the Dhamma shown by you, my Cambodian brothers and sisters. Your kusala in the past conditions your interest in listening to the Dhamma today. You are listening, because you know that the Dhamma is your true refuge. We can listen at this moment, because kamma is the condition that our life still continues, from one moment to the next moment, wherever we are. The moment of seeing or hearing something pleasant, wherever we are in Cambodia or somewhere else, is the result of kusala kamma. However, more important than pleasant experiences through the senses is the fact that you, conditioned by listening to the Dhamma in the past, have confidence today to go on listening and to develop right understanding. In this way the characteristics of realities which appear now can be understood as they are. Nothing else in the world is more valuable than the Triple Gem which is our true refuge.

Buth Sawong: Should we drive defilements away or should we flee from defilements?

Sujin: Defilements accompany the citta, they have been accumulated. No matter to where you flee, defilements will always go with you. Where there is citta there are defilements. But when the citta is kusala, when there is paññā, there are no lobha, dosa or moha; there are at that moment no defilements which cause dukkha.

Buth Sawong: What should I do to overcome defilements?

Sujin: Do you believe that you can overcome defilements yourself? Or should you develop right understanding, paññā, which performs the function of eradicating defilements?

Buth Sawong: Some people ask what they should do to attain nibbāna.

Sujin: At this moment nibbāna does not appear. You are seeing or hearing now. When you have penetrated the characteristics of the realities which are appearing now, clinging to these realities can be eliminated. When paññā has been developed to the degree that enlightenment can be attained, the citta turns away from conditioned realities which arise and fall away, it has no inclination to experience them; it turns towards the unconditioned reality, to nibbāna. At the moment of enlightenment paññā is lokuttara paññā, supramundane paññā.

Buth Sawong: People have questions about the different degrees of the state of the sotāpanna, of people who have reached the first stage of enlightenment. Different sotāpannas have a different number of rebirths and different kinds of rebirths.

Sujin: This depends on the strength of paññā of the sotāpanna. If he has a high degree of paññā he will be reborn only once. If he has a lesser degree of paññā he will be reborn more than once, but, according to the scriptures, the sotāpanna cannot be reborn more than seven times[22].

Buth Sawong: How can there be different degrees of the paññā which penetrates the four noble Truths at the moment of enlightenment? Can a distinction be made between paññā of a lesser degree and of a higher degree?

---

[22] The sotāpanna has to continue to develop paññā in order to attain higher stages of enlightenment. When the stage of the arahat has been reached there will be no more rebirth. This means the end of dukkha.

Sujin: This can be compared with the passing of an examination by different students. They all pass the examination, but some have high marks and others have low marks, depending on their different degrees of knowledge and capacity. Even so, when enlightenment is attained, the paññā of different people has different degrees, but be it of a lesser degree or of a higher degree, it penetrates the four noble Truths.

Chapter 4

Listening to the Dhamma
Dhamma Discussion with Cambodians in Nakorn Nāyok (Thailand) (Part One)

Sujin: I wish to pay my deepest respect to the venerable bhikkhu who is present here. I am so happy that you all have come here for a discussion on the Dhamma. For a discussion on the Dhamma I should not be the only person who speaks, but different people should take part in the discussion. If there are problems and questions concerning the Dhamma, please, let us discuss these now, because our time is limited.

Interpreter: We do not dare to ask questions yet.

Sujin: If there are no questions yet, I would like to speak about the Triple Gem, about the meaning of taking refuge in the Triple Gem[23]. As we all know, we take our refuge in the Exalted One, the Buddha, the Fully Enlightened One. We take refuge in his wisdom, his purity, and his compassion. Taking refuge in the Buddha seems nothing extraordinary. However, if people do not study and if they do not have profound understanding of the meaning of the Buddha's wisdom, purity and compassion, they pay respect only in a superficial way, they follow only what they know about these qualities from hearsay. If we want to know what the Buddha's wisdom, purity and compassion really are, we should study and investigate the Dhamma. If people have not studied the Dhamma, they do not really know what it means that the Buddha was a person without defilements.

There must be a way leading to the eradication of defilements. After the Buddha attained enlightenment, he showed this

[23] The three Gems of the Buddha, the Dhamma and the Sangha.

way to others. Therefore, we must really understand what the Dhamma is the Buddha penetrated at the attainment of enlightenment and taught to others as well. The Dhamma is something people cannot conceive by themselves. The Buddha accumulated the excellent qualities which are the "perfections" for four incalculable periods of time and a hundred thousand aeons, in order to realize at the attainment of enlightenment the true Dhamma (sacca dhamma). Thus he was able to teach the Dhamma to others as well.

We should have right understanding of the word "sacca dhamma", true Dhamma, the Dhamma which is the truth. Nobody can change the nature of that which is true, that which is real. There is at this moment dhamma, that which is true or real. If we do not study the teachings, we may try to find the true dhamma somewhere else, but if we study what the Buddha taught we will know that at this very moment there is true dhamma, dhamma which is real, and everybody can verify for himself the truth of dhamma. Everybody who is born has eyes, ears, nose, tongue, bodysense and mind. It is through eyes, ears, nose, tongue, bodysense and mind that we can know dhammas, realities. If there were no seeing, hearing, smelling, tasting, the experience of tangible object and thinking, nobody could know that there are dhammas, realities. Since realities are known because of the experiences through the senses and the mind, we do not have to look for dhamma somewhere else. Seeing at this moment is dhamma, it is a reality which sees. In the Tipiṭaka the Buddha explains the truth of seeing, hearing, smelling, tasting, the experience of tangible object and thinking. At this moment there is already dhamma, but because of ignorance we are not able to understand that there are dhammas, not self. Therefore, we have to listen to the teachings of the Buddha who explains that everything is dhamma.

The dhamma which appears through eyes at this moment appears because it has arisen. If it had not arisen it could not appear. The dhamma which is sound appearing through the ears, is dhamma which has arisen. If it had not arisen it could not appear. Whatever arises must have conditions for its arising, and after it has arisen it falls away again. Someone who has developed paññā, understanding, is able to realize through direct experience the characteristic of impermanence, the arising and falling away of realities appearing through eyes, ears, nose, tongue, bodysense and mind. He can directly understand that everything in and around him is dhamma which arises and then falls away.

If one listens to the teachings one can have theoretical understanding of realities. When there is seeing, one can understand that this is a reality which arises and then falls away. When there is hearing, one can understand that this is a reality which arises and then falls away. If the realities appearing through eyes, ears, nose, tongue, bodysense and mind are not dhammas, where else can dhamma be found?

In order to be able to understand and to become familiar with dhammas one should, by listening to the teachings, learn more about the things which are real and which are appearing. In this way people will very gradually acquire more understanding of realities. Generally people are inclined to think of the result which is far off, namely the penetration of the noble Truths, the direct experience of the characteristic of nibbāna. However, if one does not know the characteristic of the dhamma which appears right now, one will not be able to realize the characteristic of nibbāna. At this moment the characteristic of nibbāna does not appear, but the reality which can be experienced through eyes appears. The reality which can be experienced through ears appears, it arises and then falls away, time and again. Therefore it is important to remember that we should investigate and study the Buddha's teachings. The Dhamma he taught is about all realities which can be experienced in daily life through eyes, ears, nose, tongue, bodysense and mind. If we listen to the Dhamma we can gradually come to understand the characteristics of the realities which are appearing right now. We will not merely have theoretical understanding acquired by thinking about them, but we will have understanding of the characteristics of the realities which appear.

Theoretical knowledge about realities is quite different from direct understanding of the characteristics of realities which are appearing. These are two different levels of understanding. We may, for example, speak now about seeing as a reality, a kind of nāma which is not self, an element which experiences visible object. When someone speaks about the nature of seeing but he is not yet aware of the characteristic of seeing while there is seeing, there is merely understanding on the level of thinking, thus, theoretical understanding which stems from listening and considering what one hears. It is important to consider and investigate the Dhamma one hears, this is a necessary foundation for right understanding. The understanding which stems from listening is accumulated and this accumulated understanding is a condition for the arising of direct awareness later on. Then there can be awareness of seeing when it presents itself and at such a moment direct understanding of its characteristic can develop; seeing can be understood as a reality, as only an element, not self.

Seeing does not appear through the eyesense. The reality which sees and the reality which appears through the eyes, visible object, which is rūpa, have different characteristics which should be distinguished from each other. Seeing experiences visible object, whereas visible object does not experience anything. Visible object is a reality which contacts the eyesense and which is a condition for the arising of the citta which sees. The reality which appears through the eyes, visible object, is different from the reality which appears through the ears, sound. Sound is another reality which arises and contacts the earsense. Sound is a condition for the arising of the citta which hears. Sound is a kind of rūpa, it is different from the citta which hears. All dhammas are non-self, they are not beings or persons.

Paññā is developed by gradually understanding the characteristics of the realities which are appearing. We read in the Tipiṭaka, in the Mahā-satipaṭṭhāna sutta and also in other suttas, about the person who "lives contemplating" the characteristics of the realities which are appearing. That is, he is habitually inclined to be aware of the realities which are appearing. Not all realities appear, but all mental phenomena and physical phenomena of our life, also those which do not appear, arise and fall away. Paññā can directly understand only the realities which are appearing.

Dhammas are the realities of our daily life, and gradually one can have more understanding of them by listening to the teachings and studying them. It is important to remember that realities appear here and now, that one should not look for them somewhere else but here, or at another moment but right now. When there is awareness and understanding of the dhammas which are appearing now, paññā can come to know them as they are, as realities which arise and fall away and which are non-self. When someone merely repeats the words, "dhammas arise and fall away", there is only theoretical understanding of realities, but no direct understanding of their arising and falling away, no direct understanding of the truth.

If there are questions, please, feel free to ask them.

Interpreter: Some people wonder about the arising and falling away of realities. What arises and what falls away?

Sujin: There are now seeing and hearing. If paññā has been developed and it has become keener, it can understand directly the arising and falling away of one reality at a time. Those who have not yet studied the Dhamma or who have not considered it may only have theoretical understanding of the fact that seeing is not hearing. The development of satipaṭṭhāna is the way the Fully Enlightened One, the Buddha, and all his disciples have gone. Also Buddhists today can, in following this way, practise what the Buddha taught, even at this very moment. However, people should begin at the very beginning, that is, they should first listen to the teachings. The Buddha taught Dhamma in all details for fortyfive years to his followers, and he taught also to us today. The Buddha taught during his life, before his final passing away, Dhamma to different people with different accumulations. Even when he did not teach in detail, people could, if they had accumulated paññā, while they were listening realize the arising and falling away of realities which appeared through each of the six doorways. Realities arise and fall away, both formerly and now; they are not self, they are not beings, not persons. Someone who sincerely studies and investigates realities does not delude himself with regard to his own understanding. Although he has heard that realities arise and fall away, that they are non-self, he may not directly experience the truth. When he is sincere, he knows that he has not realized the truth; he knows that while he is seeing now, it still seems that he "sees" this or that person or thing[24]. It is necessary to be sincere with regard to the degree of one's understanding and to remember that one should continue to develop paññā so that eventually realities will be seen as they are.

Wherever and whenever we are seeing, it can be understood that seeing is only a kind of reality, an element which experiences an object, a type of nāma. There are many

[24] Person or thing are concepts one can think of; they do not impinge on the eyesense, they cannot be seen.

kinds of nāma. Seeing which experiences visible object at this moment is a kind of nāma. The citta which hears sound through the ears is another kind of nāma, different from seeing. Hearing is only an element which arises and then falls away, there is no self who hears. It can be compared to a fire which appears and is then extinguished. The fire which is extinguished has completely disappeared, it did not go anywhere else. The reality which arises now and then falls away has disappeared completely. It is not in accordance with the truth to take what has fallen away and disappeared for self or mine. During our whole life from birth until this moment there is no single reality which, after it had arisen, did not fall away. All realities are like a fire which originates and is then extinguished; they do not last and they are non-self. Hearing which has arisen just for a short moment has fallen away. The hearing of this moment is different from the hearing of a previous moment. The hearing of a previous moment is nowhere to be found. There is no self who hears, hearing is only a reality, a kind of element which arises, hears and then falls away completely. Realities arise and fall away in succession; they are succeeding one another until the last moment of this life, the moment of dying. We all know that death is departure, that it is the severance, the separation from everything; at death there is nothing left of our life in this world. It is the same with hearing which previously arose; it has fallen away completely, there is nothing left of it, it has "died". In the teachings the expression "momentary death" (khaṇika maraṇa) has been used. If we understand the meaning of this term we will see that there is death of each reality which has arisen and then fallen away completely. One does not have to wait until the approaching of death with developing understanding that there is nothing left of "ourselves". Paññā should realize "momentary death", namely, the arising and falling away of realities at this moment. In this way the wrong view which takes realities for "mine", self, beings or persons can be eradicated. We should gradually develop understanding of the characteristics of the realities which appear at this moment. Otherwise we will remain only on the level of theoretical understanding; we will merely remember the words of the Buddha's teaching about the impermanence of dhammas and their nature of non-self.

Everybody here would like to know in what way he can penetrate the truth of the realities which are now arising and falling away and which are non-self. The Buddha showed the one and only way to realize the truth, and that is: awareness of the characteristics of realities which are appearing at this moment. People have heard about the term "sati", awareness or mindfulness, but this does not mean that they understand the characteristic of sati. One should listen to the Dhamma so that one can understand that sati is a sobhana (beautiful) dhamma. Sati is different from thinking (vitakka). Thinking can be kusala, wholesome, or akusala, unwholesome, and when there is unwholesome thinking there is no sati. We should know that sati is a sobhana cetasika (mental factor) which is heedful, aware of what is wholesome. We listen to the Dhamma at this moment, and if there comes to be more understanding of realities, it is due to sati which is aware, heedful with regard to what has been heard. When someone, however, is drowsy, takes no interest in the Dhamma, and thinks of something else, the citta is not kusala citta and thus there is no sati. From birth to death, throughout one's life, sati, thinking (vitakka) and other dhammas arise, but if one does not listen to the Dhamma which has been taught, there will be confusion about all realities. One cannot distinguish different characteristics of realities from each other and one will take them for self. Some people may use terms from the teachings they believe they have already understood, such as sati, samādhi (concentration) or paññā, but they do not know the meaning of these terms, or they give their own interpretation of them. If someone has studied the Dhamma he can have right understanding of these terms, he will know that sati is different from samādhi and different from paññā, and he will not believe that these three realities are the same. He knows that when a particular reality arises it does so depending on several conditions. Nowadays some people believe that they practise the Dhamma, but they do not know whether they have right understanding of the practice or not. The Buddha taught the Dhamma he had realized himself at the moment of enlightenment, so that those who listened could also develop paññā themselves. This shows the Buddha's incomparable compassion towards his followers. If someone teaches Dhamma it may happen that those who listen do not acquire any understanding from what they hear. If paññā does not arise as a result of listening to the Dhamma the listening is not helpful. Buddhists pay respect to the Buddha because he taught them the Dhamma in such a way that they could develop paññā themselves and penetrate the four noble Truths. When people listen to the Dhamma and they understand what has been taught, there will be paññā which knows in what way the Dhamma should be practised. There is no self who practises, there are only different realities, dhammas. Sati is not self, it is a particular kind of dhamma. Samādhi is another kind of dhamma and paññā is again another kind of dhamma. If there is no right understanding of what sati, samādhi and paññā are, people will mistakenly believe that they are practising the Dhamma.

In the scriptures, the Tipiṭaka, the Buddha taught what the right Path is and what the wrong Path. A person who has studied the Dhamma and who has right understanding of it knows which way of practice is the wrong Path and which the right Path. He knows that the right Path is the development of paññā which penetrates the true nature of the realities which are appearing. If someone believes that he can practise the Dhamma without understanding the realities which are appearing he is definitely on the wrong way. Thus, the wrong Path is the practice without the development of paññā whereas the right Path is the practice which is the development of right understanding of realities.

If paññā does not arise one does not know in what way the characteristic of samādi, concentration, is different from sati and from paññā, and then one is on the wrong Path. From the beginning we should know whether we practise the Dhamma at this moment or not. If someone believes that he cannot practise the Dhamma at this moment, he does not follow the teachings as contained in the Tipiṭaka. Those who have penetrated the noble Truths have done so in their ordinary daily lives. Paññā can penetrate whatever reality arises naturally in daily life. However, if there is no paññā the truth of this moment cannot be understood. The Dhamma the Buddha taught is not something separate from our ordinary daily life; the Buddha taught the truth about what appears through eyes, ears, nose, tongue, bodysense and mind, about lobha, dosa, kusala and mettā (loving kindness). The Buddha taught about all realities in detail.

We should understand in what way sati is different from samādhi. People are often confused as to these two realities, they take samādhi for sati. They mistakenly believe that they should concentrate on particular realities and that is the right Path. If someone develops the way leading to the realisation of the noble Truths he knows that at this moment sati can arise naturally in daily life. So long as there is no right understanding of the Dhamma there is no foundation for the right practice, and therefore, it would be better not to try to practise at all.

All those who were disciples of the Buddha had listened to the Dhamma. The degree of their understanding of the Dhamma was dependant on the extent they had accumulated the "perfections". If they had a great deal of understanding, right mindfulness, sammā-sati, could be aware of the characteristics of realities and in this way their true nature could be penetrated in accordance with the Buddha's teaching.

Chapter 5

Different Degrees of Understanding
Dhamma Discussion with Cambodians in Nakorn Nāyok (Part Two)

Sujin: We should know the dhammas as they appear in daily life. For example, is there dhamma when we are laughing?

Interpreter: There is dhamma, there is no person who laughs.

Sujin: There are different feelings (in Pāli: vedanā). When we do not laugh what kind of feeling is there?

Interpreter: There can be indifferent feeling, upekkhā vedanā.

Sujin: We know the names of all the different feelings: pleasant bodily feeling, painful bodily feeling, happy feeling, unhappy feeling and indifferent feeling. People may only know their names. But when a particular feeling appears and there is awareness of its characteristic, feeling will be known as it is. Through awareness the different characteristics of different feelings will be known and understood as they are.

There is, for example, indifferent feeling at this moment of seeing[25]. After seeing has fallen away happy feeling can arise together with attachment, lobha, and that moment is different from seeing[26]. When we are enjoying pleasant things there must be happy feeling which accompanies lobha-mūla-citta, citta rooted in attachment. Whereas, when we listen to the Dhamma and we are happy that we hear things we had not heard before, there is happy feeling accompanying

[25] Seeing, hearing, smelling and tasting are vipākacittas (cittas which are results of kamma) , which are accompanied by indifferent feeling.
[26] Lobha can be accompanied by happy feeling or by indifferent feeling.

kusala citta[27]. This kind of happy feeling is different from the happy feeling accompanying lobha-mūla-citta. Realities have each their own nature, their own characteristic, and paññā is able to know the true nature of different characteristics of realities when they are appearing.

Do you think that this is difficult to understand, or easy?

Interpreter: It is difficult.

Sujin: That is true. If someone believes that it is easy he deludes himself. The Buddha, the Fully Enlightened One, did certainly not teach a Dhamma which would be easy to understand.

When paññā can penetrate the true nature of realities it will be known that realities change extremely rapidly. Feelings change all the time. We all have moments that we feel unhappy, sad, discontented and depressed on account of our thoughts. At the moment of seeing there is no thinking, but after seeing has fallen away thinking can arise. Some people have unhappy thoughts, others have happy thoughts. Because of the Buddha's teachings we can come to know the true nature of the realities of our daily life, and thus we can see that his teachings are of immense benefit. We can verify the truth of his teachings ourselves. We all can find out, for example, that a moment of grief is different from seeing which is accompanied by indifferent feeling. Different realities should be distinguished from each other. Happy feeling or unhappy feeling can arise after seeing or hearing, they do not arise at the moment of seeing or hearing. If we gradually come to know the true nature of realities, ignorance and the suffering due to ignorance can eventually be overcome. If paññā realizes the truth of realities more deeply, that is, if it knows them as only dhammas which arise and fall away and which are non-self, the suffering which arises

---

[27] Kusala citta can be accompanied by happy feeling or by indifferent feeling.

on account of our thoughts will become less. To the extent that paññā has become developed our suffering will decrease.

Paññā which is of the level of theoretical understanding, conditioned by listening to the Dhamma, is quite different from paññā which is developed through awareness of nāma and rūpa. The latter kind of paññā is again different from the paññā which penetrates the true nature of realities at the attainment of enlightenment. The paññā of those who attain enlightenment is of different levels in accordance with the four different stages which are attained. The paññā which penetrates the four noble Truths at the attainment of the stage of the sotāpanna, the streamwinner, is of a level which is different from the degree of paññā which penetrates the four noble Truths at the attainment of the stage of the sakadāgāmī, the once-returner; the paññā of the stage of the anāgāmī, the non-returner, and the paññā of the stage of the arahat, the perfected one, are again different degrees of paññā[28].

Those who are followers of the Buddha should have great patience in order to listen to the Dhamma and consider what they heard, and in this way there can be more understanding of realities. This cannot be achieved by going somewhere else in order to follow a particular practice. If one is truly patient sati and paññā can very gradually develop. Moreover, we should be truthful as to our development of paññā. If there is still ignorance of realities we should realize this and not mistakenly believe that we know realities already. We should not delude ourselves, taking for paññā what is not paññā. So long as the realities which are appearing through the six doors are not known as they are, there is no right understanding which can only be developed by the right practice. Those who follow the Buddha's teachings

[28] Defilements are progressively eradicated at the attainment of the different stages of enlightenment, and at the attainment of arahatship all of them are eradicated.

must start in the right way from the beginning. When they are listening to the Dhamma they should do so for the right purpose, and this is: the understanding of realities as they are. The goal is not gain, honour, fame or praise; the goal is not to be esteemed by others as a person who has a great deal of paññā. From the beginning, paññā should be developed for the right purpose, it should not be developed with clinging to the understanding of the four noble Truths.

Someone who develops paññā should be sincere with regard to himself: he should know whether there is already understanding of the characteristic of the reality which is appearing at this moment or not yet. If there is not yet such understanding he should continue to listen to the Dhamma and consider again and again what he has heard, and he should continue to develop sati and paññā.

Nobody knows when he will die, when he will have to take leave of everything in this world. If we do not develop paññā the clinging we have accumulated will have the opportunity to arise again and again, also in future lives, and it will become firm and obstinate. Therefore, what is most valuable in our life is paññā which knows realities as they are. Paññā is the only factor which can eradicate defilements. We should see the invaluable benefit of paññā which is conditioned by listening to the Dhamma and which is able to understand realities more and more. Paññā should be developed without having expectations as to the moment when the four noble Truths will be penetrated. If one begins to gradually understand realities one is on the way leading to the penetration of the four noble Truths, to the experience of nibbāna at the attainment of enlightenment. There is no other way leading to this goal. One should not mistakenly believe that something else should be known but what appears in daily life. It is essential to remember this. The right Path is knowing realities as they naturally appear at this moment. If someone wants to know something else, if he does not develop understanding of the reality which naturally appears at this moment, he walks the wrong way.

Interpreter: Some people wonder about the meaning of dukkha. In the scriptures sometimes the term dukkha sacca, the truth of dukkha, is used and sometimes the term dukkha ariya sacca, the noble Truth of dukkha. They wonder whether the dukkha of the ariyans, the noble persons who have attained enlightenment, is different from the dukkha of ordinary people.

Sujin: The realities which arise and fall away are dukkha and nobody can change this truth. The term dukkha sacca or dukkha ariya sacca refers to one of the three characteristics of conditioned realities, namely their arising and falling away[29]. Nobody can prevent the reality which has arisen from falling away again. The characteristic of the reality which arises and falls away is dukkha, because arising and falling away is suffering, not happiness. All people want happiness which lasts, which continues forever and which does not fall away, but conditioned realities have the characteristic of dukkha, because they arise and then fall away immediately. There are three characteristics common to all conditioned realities, namely: the characteristic of impermanence, that is, the arising and falling away, the characteristic of dukkha, suffering or unsatisfactoriness, since what arises and falls away cannot be happiness, and the characteristic of anattā, non-self. There is no self who can exert control over realities, because they are as they are, according to their own nature.

Interpreter: People are still confused as to the terms dukkha sacca, the truth of dukkha, and dukkha ariya sacca, the noble truth of dukkha. They believe that the first term refers to dukkha of ordinary people and the latter term to dukkha of the ariyans. I myself understand that dukkha ariya sacca,

---

[29] These three characteristics are: impermanence, dukkha and anattā, non-self.

the noble Truth of dukkha is the first one of the four noble Truths, whereas dukkha sacca, the truth of dukkha, refers to dukkha as one of the three general characteristics common to all conditioned realities.

Sujin: Dukkha sacca, one of the three characteristics common to all conditioned realities, is nothing else but dukkha, suffering, due to the arising and falling away of realities. The person who has directly realized and penetrated the three characteristics of realities is an ariyan, a person who has attained enlightenment. He has directly realized the truth through his own experience, he has realized the arising and falling away of realities, and this is different from merely repeating that all realities which arise and fall away are dukkha. A person may repeat these words without directly experiencing the arising and falling away of realities.

Dukkha sacca is the truth of dukkha, and what is true does not depend on whether a person understands and realizes it or not. Nobody can change the truth of dukkha. The person who has realized by his own experience the truth of dukkha is an ariyan. Therefore, also the term dukkha ariya sacca, the noble truth of dukkha, is used, which is the truth of the ariyans, the enlightened ones, the truth realized by the ariyans.

Interpreter: Some people wonder whether it is true that there are three levels of being a buddhist, namely, the beginning, the middle and the end. They believe that the beginning is the taking of refuge in the Buddha, the Dhamma and the Sangha[30]. They believe that the middle is, in short, wholesome conduct, and that the end is the realisation of the four noble Truths. Some people have wrong view, they do not take their refuge in the Triple Gem nor do they have wholesome conduct; they steal in order to obtain food. However, they still come to listen to the preaching of Dhamma

[30] The sangha means the order of monks, but as one of the three refuges it is the ariyan sangha, the community of enlightened ones.

in the temple and it is said that they then can become enlightened. I am puzzled and I wonder whether this is possible or not.

Sujin: When people have listened to the Dhamma and grasped what they heard, they will understand who the Fully Enlightened One, the Buddha, really is. So long as people have not studied the Dhamma, they may just pay respect to the Buddha statue, but they may do so without any understanding of who the Buddha is. Those who have listened to the Dhamma will know that there is no other person except the Buddha who taught the truth of the Dhamma, which they can verify for themselves and realize through their own experience.

When people listen to the Dhamma and consider what they heard they can acquire right understanding of realities which appear now, such as seeing and hearing. They can understand that at the moment of seeing there cannot be hearing, and that seeing has to fall away before hearing can arise. They can verify that the characteristic of thinking is different again from seeing and hearing. Some people who listen to the Dhamma are not able to understand it, whereas others who listen understand what they hear, they understand immediately that there is no self, that there are only different realities. It depends on the extent to which someone has accumulated the "perfection" of paññā, whether he is able to understand the Dhamma he hears and can develop paññā to such a degree that it can penetrate the true characteristics of realities and even realize the four noble Truths. When the Buddha, before his final passing away, explained the Dhamma, some people could, even while they listened, realize the four noble Truths and become arahats. Some people reached the third stage of enlightenment, the stage of the anāgāmī, non-returner, others the second stage, the stage of the sakadāgāmī, once-returner, and others again the first stage, the stage of the sotāpanna, streamwinner. King

Bimbisara and the people of his retinue, for example, attained enlightenment to the degree of the sotāpanna. There were also people who listened but did not attain any stage of enlightenment. It depends on the degree of a person's understanding whether he can penetrate the true nature of the characteristics of realities or not. Those who listen to the Dhamma and understand what they hear can truly take their refuge in the Triple Gem. They know that there is nobody else but the Buddha, the Fully Enlightened One, who can teach the Dhamma.

Interpreter: The Buddhists who have come here to listen to the Dhamma are full of enthusiasm and joy, they are so happy that they can meet you, Ācariya[31] Sujin. Some people wonder whether they, although they have not first undertaken five or eight precepts[32], can, after listening to the Dhamma, practise it and develop insight, vipassanā. Or do they first have to take their refuge in the Triple Gem and observe the moral precepts for a long time?

People who ask such questions are confused about these matters, they have not applied themselves much to the study of the Dhamma. They like to use this opportunity to ask their questions so that they can hear your answer and gain more understanding.

Sujin: Anumodana[33], I appreciate the interest of all people here. In this present time it is normal that Buddhists find it difficult to study and understand the Tipiṭaka. Therefore, they are generally inclined to give their own interpretation to the Buddhist teachings and they believe that they have right understanding of the texts of the Tipiṭaka. However, the Buddha's teachings are subtle and deep, and nobody can understand the truth just by himself.

---

[31] The Pāli term for teacher.

[32] Rules of wholesome conduct.

[33] This is the Pāli term for thanksgiving or satisfaction. By this word one's appreciation of someone else's good deeds is expressed.

Interpreter: Is there a method by which sati can be aware of realities appearing through the eyes, ears, nose, tongue, body and mind? How can sati arise fast enough in order to be aware of the present moment?

Sujin: There is no method which can be followed, but at this moment realities are appearing already. One can begin to develop more understanding of them. If one first listens to the Dhamma and understands what one hears, sati can arise and be aware of realities. However, we have to listen again and again in order to gain more understanding of realities as non-self. What appears through the eyes, visible object, has contacted the rūpa which is eyesense; it just appears for an extremely short moment and then it falls away. If we gain more understanding of realities we will not forget that rūpa-kkhandha (the khandha of physical phenomena), vedanā-kkhandha (feelings), saññā-kkhandha (remembrance or "perception"), saṅkhāra-kkhandha (formations or activities, all cetasikas other than vedanā and saññā) and viññāṇa-kkhandha (consciousness), thus, the five khandhas, are not self, not "I". Listening conditions the accumulation of sati and paññā, and thus, awareness of the reality which appears can arise and at that moment understanding of it can develop. This is in fact satipaṭṭhāna. Satipaṭṭhāna is not a particular method which should be followed in order to be aware of realities. Satipaṭṭhāna is the development of the understanding of the characteristics of realities which arise and appear, each because of their own conditions.

Do you know ahead of time when realities such as hearing, anger or sati will arise? If there are not the right conditions for hearing we cannot cause its arising. Only when there are conditions for it, it arises. Even so, when there are not the right conditions for the arising of sati, we cannot cause its arising. When there are the right conditions for sati, it arises and then we will know that there is no self who can cause its arising.

The development of satipaṭṭhāna is very subtle; if there is no right understanding of its development people will cling to wrong practice (sīlabbata parāmāsa kāya-gantha). Only paññā can eradicate wrong practice. When someone does not know the difference between the moment when there is sati and the moment when there is no sati, he may try to follow another way which is the wrong practice. Right understanding of the way how to develop satipaṭṭhāna is indispensable; paññā should know that sati is anattā, non-self, and it should know when there is sati and when there is forgetfulness of realities. If the difference between such moments is not known paññā cannot be developed. There will be clinging to the concept of self who tries to "do" something.

The way to begin is knowing when sati arises and when there is forgetfulness. I will give an example. We all touch things which are hard. Even a child knows that something is hard, because hardness impinges on the rūpa which is bodysense and there is citta which experiences the characteristic of hardness. This happens time and again in daily life. When we just experience or notice hardness, it does not mean that there is sati and paññā. Someone, however, who has listened to the Dhamma knows that hardness is a reality which appears when it contacts the rūpa which is bodysense. Hardness is non-self, there is nobody who can create the element of hardness. Whenever the bodysense, which is all over the body, from head to toes, is contacted by something hard, the element of hardness appears. The true characteristic of that particular element presents itself at such a moment. However, when there is forgetfulness of realities and there is no right understanding, we take the whole body, from head to toes, for self.

From the time we have been getting up in the morning until now we have, time and again, touched what is hard, but if one has not listened to the Dhamma one is forgetful of such moments. A person who has listened to the Dhamma and has grasped what he heard, has right understanding of the characteristic of hardness when it appears. He understands that it is only a reality which appears, not a "self".

Just a moment ago we experienced something hard, and now, at this moment, we can begin to understand that hardness is only a reality. Such understanding is due to sati which has arisen and which is aware of the characteristic of hardness. When sati arises it is aware of a reality just for an extremely short moment, and after that there is again forgetfulness of realities, we are thinking of other things.

Chapter 6

The Eightfold Path
Dhamma Discussion with Cambodians in Nakorn Nāyok (Part Three)

Sujin: When the Buddha explained about realities such as seeing and visible object which is experienced through the eyes, and the listeners understood the characteristic of sati, they could know whether there was mindfulness while seeing, or forgetfulness. When the Buddha explained about hearing and sound, the listeners knew, when sati arose, whether there was mindfulness of the characteristic of sound or of hearing, the reality which experiences sound. The Dhamma I am referring to now is the Dhamma the Buddha taught in the Jeta Grove, in the Bamboo Grove and in other places. If we go back to the Buddha's time, more than two thousand five hundred years ago, the Dhamma I refer to now was true also for people at that time. If people at that time were not forgetful of realities, they could penetrate their true nature. Some people could during the explanation of realities penetrate the truth, and others could do so after a more detailed explanation[34], but today there are no such people. Even after listening to an explanation about seeing it is not sure that there will be awareness of it. We should develop precise understanding of the realities appearing through

---

[34] The first kind of people are called in Pāli: ugghaṭitaññū, and the second kind: vipacitaññū. The first and the second kind of people attain enlightenment quickly, they cannot be found today. There are also people who penetrate the truth after having asked questions and considered the Dhamma for a longer period of time, and they are called: neyya puggala, people who need guidance. Those who, although they heard much and considered much, do not attain enlightenment are called pada-parama, which means: those whose highest attainment are the words (of the texts).

the six doors and we should know whether there is mindfulness of those realities or not yet. People should investigate with regard to themselves when there is forgetfulness of realities and when there is sati. They should understand that when sati does not arise it is impossible to know as they are the realities which are appearing. It is impossible to force the arising of sati, but paññā can be developed little by little if one is sincere as to one's own development and knows for oneself whether there is sati or forgetfulness. This is daily life and people should know their daily life.

The Buddha taught the development of the eightfold Path and this consists of eight factors which are the following cetasikas:

right understanding or sammā-diṭṭhi

right thinking or sammā-sankappa

right speech or sammā-vācā

right bodily action or sammā-kammanta

right livelihood or sammā-ājīva

right effort or sammā-vāyāma

right mindfulness or sammā-sati

right concentration or sammā-samādhi

Right understanding and right thinking are the supporting factors which constitute the wisdom of the eightfold Path[35]. Right speech, right action and right livelihood are the supporting factors which constitute the sīla, morality, of the eightfold Path[36]. Right effort, right mindfulness and right

---

[35] Right thinking has the function of "touching" the nāma or rūpa which appears, it assists right understanding so that it can know its true nature.

[36] These three cetasikas have the function of abstaining from wrong speech, wrong action and wrong livelihood. When enlightenment is attained they have the function of eradicating the causes of wrong speech, wrong action and wrong livelihood.

concentration are the supporting factors which constitute the concentration or calm of the eightfold Path[37]. Thus, there are sīla, samādhi (calm) and paññā of the eightfold Path.

When there is right mindfulness of a reality there is at that moment "training" in higher sīla, higher citta (concentration or calm) and higher paññā[38]. These three kinds of "training" are called "higher training", because they are training of a higher degree, more subtle and refined than other kinds of training. At the moment someone performs akusala kamma there is ignorance of lobha, dosa and moha. When sati arises it can be aware of akusala, even when there is only a slight degree of lobha which does not have the intensity of akusala kamma; sati can be aware of the true characteristic of that reality. This is the higher training in sīla, morality, because even a slight degree of akusala is realized.

As regards samādhi, concentration, this is ekaggatā cetasika, the reality which is focusing on the object which is experienced; it conditions citta to experience only one object. There is wrong concentration, micchā-samādi, accompanying akusala citta, and right concentration, sammā-samādi,

---

[37] Concentration has the function of focussing on one object and it arises with each citta. As regards right concentration of the eightfold Path, when there is awareness of a nāma or rūpa, sammā-samādhi has the function of focussing on that one object so that right understanding can understand it as it is. As regards right effort, this is the cetasika viriya, energy or effort. It has the function of strenghtening the citta and accompanying cetasikas, so that they can perform their functions. Right effort strengthens the other factors, so that there is courage and perseverance with the development of right understanding.

[38] When there is mindfulness of realities appearing through six doors there is restraint of the six doors, there is no opportunity for akusala. This also means that there is calm at that moment. Sati can prevent one from committing akusala kamma and also from akusala which is of a lesser degree. Thus, at the moment of right mindfulness there is the threefold higher training: training in higher sīla, higher calm and higher paññā. Training is the translation of the Pāli term sikkhā. Training means applying oneself again and again.

accompanying kusala citta. Whenever sati arises and is aware of the characteristics of realities, sammā-samādhi focuses on the object of mindfulness. At that very moment understanding of that object can develop, and gradually the characteristics of realities can be known as they are.

The development of paññā is a kind of mental development which takes a great deal of time because sati does not often arise in a day, it does not arise as frequently as akusala citta. Sati arises very seldom, but when it arises and it is aware of realities, paññā can gradually have more understanding of them. When there is forgetfulness again, there is ignorance which does not know realities as they are. Every day there are many moments of ignorance and thus, a great deal of ignorance is accumulated, whereas sati and paññā can only be accumulated little by little.

Right understanding is able to penetrate the true characteristics of all realities. When a person has realized the arising and falling away of realities, there can gradually be the elimination of the wrong view that realities are self, and then he can, at the attainment of enlightenment, penetrate the four noble Truths. The person who has penetrated the noble Truths at the attainment of the first stage of enlightenment is the streamwinner, sotāpanna. At that moment, the characteristic of nibbāna is experienced and doubt and wrong view of realities are eradicated.

The sotāpanna knows that he is not a once-returner, sakadāgāmī, who has realized the second stage of enlightenment, nor a no-returner, anāgāmī, who has realized the third stage, nor an arahat, the perfected one who has eradicated all defilements. The paññā of the degree of the sotāpanna cannot eradicate lobha, dosa and moha. There are still accumulated conditions for the arising of akusala dhammas, other than the ones he has eradicated. Therefore, the sotāpanna has to continue developing paññā in the way he used to, and this is: awareness of the characteristics of realities which are naturally appearing in his daily life. This is the only way to reach the goal, there is no other way.

Interpreter: What is the meaning of the expression: fixing one's attention in order to know realities in time?

Sujin: This is clinging to the idea that realities are self. When sati does not arise and there is forgetfulness of realities, one takes realities for a "thing" which exists. For example, when there is seeing, people believe that they see a temple hall, persons and different things which seem to exist. Whereas when there is paññā it realizes that what appears through the eyesense are not people or different things but only visible object, a kind of element which appears through the eyesense. When we close our eyes that which was seen is no longer there; we can still think of people who are sitting, we can remember them, but such moments are different from the moments of seeing visible object which appears through eyesense. If someone closes his eyes and all the people would leave the temple hall, he might believe that there are still people inside the temple hall. This shows that the moments of thinking of concepts is altogether different from the actual seeing. Realities arise and fall away, succeeding one another very rapidly. The realities which alternately appear through eyes, ears, nose, tongue, bodysense and mind are taken as a "whole", a person or a particular thing. We should not try to fix our attention on a reality at a certain moment in order to know it "in time", that is impossible. It is sati itself which is aware of the characteristic of the reality which is appearing, one characteristic at a time, until it is clearly understood, until it appears as non-self.

Interpreter: The listeners would like to know more about the personal life of Achāriya Sujin: her education, her work, also her work with regard to the explanation of the Buddhist teachings. They would like to know about these things, no matter in short or in detail. I would like to be the interviewer.

Is Achāriya from Bangkok?

Sujin: I do not know whether I can say that I am from Bangkok. My father worked in the Forestry Department and his children were born in the province where he lived. I was born in Ubonrajadhani, but I had my education in Saint Mary's school in Bangkok. I lived during my childhood in Bangkok until I finished the sixth class of the Secondary School. After that I passed the entrance examination to a school of preparatory education for Chulalongkorn University. Then I enlisted at that University and studied there until the second year. However, I did not finish my study there. Since I often missed lectures about important subjects and did not study regularly, I failed twice my examinations and finally had to leave the University. I then went to stay with my father who was at that time at the Forestry Department in Chiangmai. His children usually went to school from their early childhood in Bangkok, where they had someone to take care of them, since my mother had passed away when we were still very young. In vacation time we would visit my father in the province. When my older sister had become a bachelor of arts, she started to teach at the Prince Royal School in Chiangmai. I was given a special permit to teach at the Dara School, near the Prince Royal School. When my father left the government service and returned to Bangkok, we followed him and also went to live in Bangkok.

Someone encouraged me to teach Thai to foreigners at the Thai Language Department of the Missionary School and there I taught for a long time. After that I left this school together with some friends and we founded our own school, namely the Thai Language School Association. Later on the school was moved from the building where it originally was to another one near my house in Sathorn. Finally my father sold this house were we had lived for more than forty years, and then we moved near my younger sister's house in Soy Patthanavet (Sukhumvit 91). Since this was far away from the school I stopped teaching and delegated the teaching to friends, so that they together would continue this work.

Interpreter: Where did you first study the Dhamma?

Sujin: I started with the study of the Abhidhamma. I came across an announcement in the newspaper the "Bangkok World", explaining that the Buddhist Association had started classes for the study of Buddhism and thereupon I began to study with Achāriya Neb Mahāniranan and with others who were members of an association of teachers of Dhamma. I mostly studied in the class of Achāriya Neb. At that time I was still working, but only half a day, and the rest of the day I spent reviewing what I had learnt from the Abhidhamma teaching on Sunday. Before 1957 there was not yet a translation of the Tipiṭaka from Pāli into Thai, there were only a few textbooks on Buddhism in Thai. After 1957, when there were translations available, I started to study the Thai translations of the Tipiṭaka and other books such as the Visuddhimagga ("Path of Purification")[39]. I visited Achāriya Neb almost every Thursday and when I had doubts about certain topics I asked her opinion. She explained such topics to me with great kindness. Whenever she wanted me to accompany her and help her to explain the Dhamma I went with her, no matter the occasion was a cremation ceremony in the province or something else. When I had studied the Abhidhamma for two or three years, Achāriya Neb asked me to give lectures on the Dhamma in the National Cultural Institute and also in the women's prison. Whenever Achāriya Neb wanted me to do something for the propagation of Buddhism I did it to my best ability. When Achāriya Neb founded in 1963 the Research Centre on Buddhism and the Society of Spiritual Aid I lectured there as well. Later on I gave lectures in the Mahā-dhātu Temple and then in the building of Mahā-makut College Association of the Bovornivet Temple.

---

[39] An encyclopedia on Buddhism written by the great commentator Buddhaghosa, in the fifth century A.D.

Nowadays I do not give lectures any more, but I help with Dhamma discussions and I review my lectures people have heard on the radio programs. Professor Somporn gives now lectures on the "Manual of Abhidhamma" (Abhidhammattha Sangaha). At the moment I am rearranging and reviewing all the tapes, more than two thousand in number, of my programs on the different radio stations. I review them in order to make them more compact, with less repetitions.

Interpreter: You have read the Tipiṭaka and studied it. How did you acquire understanding of the development of satipaṭṭhāna from your study?

Sujin: There is no doubt that the Dhamma is our guide and therefore people should not be attached to teachers. It is very difficult to thoroughly and completely understand the Tipiṭaka, both as to the letter and the meaning, but we are able to acquire more understanding of it by listening to any person who can explain the truth of Dhamma. However, we should not accept what is not in conformity with realities. We should not cling to persons, we should not believe in persons more than in the Dhamma itself. We should really have confidence in the Dhamma the Buddha assigned as his successor, as our guide.

Everything which occurs does so because of the appropriate conditions. Nobody knows in the case of a particular person his accumulated conditions for such or such aspect of the Dhamma or for the performing of such or such task in the field of Buddhism. May everyone who has the desire to study the Dhamma help to make known the Dhamma in accordance with his own ability. If someone helps explaining the Dhamma, it is not necessary that there are many people who come to listen to him or her. People who have knowledge and understanding of the Dhamma can, each in their own way, help others who do not know the Dhamma to acquire understanding of it. There is no need to think, "I succeed this person", or, "That person succeeds me". Different people can each perform a task in the field of Dhamma, in accordance with the understanding and capability they have accumulated.

The way to make known the Dhamma is to first study it oneself, in order to have right understanding. It is wrong to expect others to study the Dhamma and not to study it oneself. Someone may say that Buddhism is most beneficial, that it gives solutions to the problems in our life and in society, but does he really study the Dhamma himself? The person who wants to study Buddhism should be quite sure when he will do so. Otherwise he will keep on thinking about the study he will do in the future, instead of actually studying the Dhamma. When a person is sure when he will study the Dhamma he should also know what exactly he will study and where, in which place, he will study. These are things people should investigate in the right way; they should not neglect studying and gaining understanding of the Dhamma themselves, they should not merely repeat what they have heard from others.

There is only one way which is the right way: everyone should be his own refuge by studying the Dhamma with the purpose to acquire more understanding of it. Everyone who studies the Dhamma and has right understanding of it, contributes to the propagation of the Dhamma, both with regard to himself and others. When people do not have right understanding of the Dhamma themselves they cannot propagate it.

Chapter 7

The Right Way and the Wrong Way
Dhamma Discussions in Pnompenh (Part One)

Buth Sawong: All people who are present here would like to hear about the development of satipaṭṭhāna. I would like to know what the difference is between the paññā which is of the level of thinking of nāma and rūpa and the paññā which penetrates the true nature of nāma and rūpa.

Sujin: First of all, people should listen to the Dhamma in order to have right understanding, to understand the truth that there are at this moment realities which are non-self. It is, however, not easy to understand that at this moment of listening to the Dhamma there is no self who listens, but that there are only realities, dhammas.

Everybody knows that he is seeing now and that seeing is real. The Buddha explained that seeing is a reality which is nāma, an element which experiences something. However, people do not realize the truth, namely that seeing experiences only what appears through the eyesense, visible object. They still believe that what is seen are this or that particular "thing".

We should listen to the Dhamma in order to have firm, well-founded understanding of realities. It seems that one sees at this moment people, flowers or a table, but one should know that the Fully Enlightened One, the Buddha, at the attainment of Buddhahood, had penetrated the true nature of realities, that he had realized that what was seen was only a reality appearing through the eyesense. This can remind us that the Dhamma which the Buddha penetrated is the truth appearing at this moment.

Although people may have listened to the Dhamma already for some time, it seems that, when their eyes are open and there is seeing which just experiences visible object, they still see different people and things as usual. This shows that there is a great deal of ignorance. Ignorance, avijjā, is the reality which does not know the characteristics of realities as they are.

Everybody here knows that he should continue to develop paññā, because paññā which is still theoretical understanding, conditioned by listening, is not able to clearly understand the true nature of realities. For the development of paññā it is important to know the difference between the moments that there is sati and the moments that there is no sati but forgetfulness of realities. When one is listening to the Dhamma there can be, because of sati which is mindful, understanding of what one hears. However, this is not the level of sati which is directly aware of the characteristic of the reality which is appearing. Listening is of great benefit if one also considers the Dhamma one has heard and thus, there can gradually be more understanding of the reality which occurs at the present moment; there can be more understanding of seeing when there is seeing. There should not be any expectation about the time when there will be clear understanding of realities. One can begin to understand that what appears through eyesense is only a kind of rūpa, visible object. Colour or visible object is conditioned by the four Great Elements, the rūpas which are solidity (the Element of Earth), cohesion (the Element of Water), heat (the Element of Fire) and motion (the Element of Wind). If there would not be these four Great Elements arising together with visible object, it could not appear[40]. Colour or visible object could not arise just by itself, as if in a vacuum. It

---

[40] Rūpas arise in groups or units of rūpas. There are different kinds of rūpas and the four Great Elements always have to arise together with each kind of rūpa. Sound, for example, could not arise without the four Great Elements.

needs the support of the four Great Elements arising together with it. Since these four Great Elements are arising together with it, we can perceive different shapes and forms. Saññā[41] can recognize these as this or that particular "thing". Saññā, remembrance, is not wrong view. Also those who have eradicated wrong view can, because of saññā, recognize what they have seen.

When sati has been developed and paññā has become keener, doubt about the difference between the characteristic of nāma, the reality which experiences an object, and the characteristic of rūpa, such as visible object appearing through eyesense, can be eradicated. But there should be a great deal of patience to listen to the Dhamma, to consider and investigate the truth that everything which appears at this moment is dhamma, reality. If sati arises it can be aware of the characteristic of whatever reality is appearing.

In the beginning there is still the idea of self. Sati may arise, but there is still a feeling of wanting or trying to understand realities. It is important to notice the difference between the moment of understanding and the moment of clinging to the understanding of realities. We should be aware of our clinging to understanding, otherwise clinging cannot be eradicated. Clinging is the origination of dukkha, and this is the second noble Truth. Clinging is the cause of not knowing the truth of realities.

We should know the purpose of listening to the Dhamma. The purpose is not obtaining something for oneself, it is not honour or fame; it is not being admired as a clever person who is full of wisdom. The purpose is knowing oneself, realizing one's lack of understanding of the characteristics of realities, one's ignorance of, for example, visible object which appears through the eyes. We should remember that what is most precious, so long as we are still alive, is paññā

---

[41] The cetasika which is remembrance, arising with each citta. Because of saññā we can recognize things.

which knows realities as they are.

If the Buddha had not taught the way to develop right understanding, we would not be able to be aware of the characteristics of realities. We would, our whole life, continue to see without knowing what the reality of seeing is. Because of the Buddha's teaching of Dhamma, people can realize for themselves when sati arises and when there is forgetfulness of realities. Nobody else can tell us whether there is sati or forgetfulness, we can know this only for ourselves. Even when sati arises, the characteristics of realities may not yet be seen as they are. However, sati can arise again and in this way there can gradually be a little more understanding of realities. One can understand that realities are appearing naturally in daily life when there are the appropriate conditions for them, and that also the reality of sati can only arise when there are conditions for it, that its arising cannot be forced. One should remember that it is sati, not self, which is aware of the characteristics of realities. Understanding this is the only way to eradicate the idea of self, the idea of, "I am practising".

The Dhamma people hear today is the Dhamma the Buddha taught in the Jeta Grove, in the Bamboo Grove and in other places. People who have listened to the Dhamma understand that seeing, hearing, thinking, happiness or sorrow are realities, dhammas. This is the true Dhamma, sacca dhamma, this is the Dhamma which is true in each life. The understanding of the true Dhamma is conditioned, it depends on whether people have heard the Dhamma in former lives. If someone during a lifespan has no opportunity to hear and understand the Dhamma, then his life is full of lobha, attachment, dosa, aversion, moha, ignorance, and other kinds of defilements, and he accumulates all the time evermore unwholesomeness. Therefore, when there is an opportunity to listen to the Dhamma, we should listen and consider it, we should also investigate for ourselves the characteristics of the realities which are appearing at this moment. We should listen again and again, and continue to investigate realities in order to develop understanding, little by little. If someone intends to develop paññā he should accumulate it from now on. If he does not begin at this moment there cannot be paññā.

I appreciate the kusala of the listeners which was accumulated in the past. This accumulation is the condition for the arising of paññā which understands the benefit of the Dhamma; it is the condition for being interested in listening to the Dhamma and applying it.

Buth Sawong: I would like to ask again what the difference is between the paññā which is theoretical understanding and the paññā which directly penetrates the truth of the Dhamma.

Sujin: At this moment people listen to the Dhamma and they understand what they hear, but this is not yet direct understanding which, when there is, for example, seeing, penetrates the true nature of this reality. Hearing appears at this moment and people know that it is a kind of nāma, hearing-consciousness (sotaviññāṇa), which arises and then falls away. They have theoretical understanding of this reality but they may not yet realize the true characteristic of the reality which hears sound, which is arising and falling away. Then there is only paññā of the level of thinking, theoretical understanding of realities. Hearing which arises at this moment is real, it is a dhamma which arises and falls away. So long as one does not directly understand the truth of the reality appearing at this moment, there is only paññā which is theoretical understanding, conditioned by listening. Whereas, when someone directly understands and penetrates the true characteristics of realities, he knows that this kind of paññā is different from theoretical understanding.

First of all, people should know the characteristic of sati.

Sati of the eightfold Path is not a "self" who is aware. Sammā-sati, right mindfulness, of the eightfold Path is aware of the reality which is appearing. When it arises there is not merely theoretical understanding. Sati is directly aware of the characteristic of the reality which is appearing, so that its true nature can be understood at that moment. Thus we can see the difference between theoretical understanding and paññā which directly understands the characteristic of the reality which is appearing. Everybody can find out for himself what level of understanding he has.

When, in the past, the Buddha taught Dhamma and explained about the six doors of the eyes, ears, nose, tongue, bodysense and mind, the listeners could, when right mindfulness arose, each for themselves realize the true nature of the realities appearing through these doorways. When sati did not arise they knew that there was only theoretical understanding which was conditioned by listening to the Dhamma.

It is paññā which can understand the characteristics of realities and we do not have to do anything special. If at this moment paññā penetrates the characteristics of realities it is not because of a self who has to make a special effort. There is no being, no person who is developing satipaṭṭhāna. When sati arises and it is aware of realities, one can know the characteristics of sati and paññā and in this way the wrong view which takes realities for self can gradually be eliminated. Finally, there can be clear understanding of the truth that everything which is appearing at this moment is dhamma. Dhammas are appearing every day through the doorways of the eyes, the ears, the nose, the tongue, the bodysense and the mind. When sati arises it is aware of realities, and if it does not arise there is ignorance which does not understand realities. Sati can be aware of the characteristics of realities which are appearing naturally, one does not have to do anything special. Paññā develops very gradually, but this way is the right way of practice.

Wanting to know something else but what appears now is useless. Realities are already appearing at this moment and thus whatever appears now can be understood as it is.

If one does not understand realities yet, one should listen again, consider again, one should learn to be aware again and again, and thus there can be more understanding. Patience and perseverance are indispensable.

The right way should be developed. Someone takes the wrong way when he wants to know something else but the reality which is appearing at this moment. Then there is no paññā. If there is paññā it must be able to understand the characteristic of the reality which is appearing now.

Those who have realized the truth can understand the great wisdom of the Buddha, they can understand that he at the attainment of enlightenment penetrated the truth of realities which are extremely difficult to understand. Realities are appearing all the time, but although one may have listened to the Dhamma for a long time, paññā may seldom arise and it may only develop very slowly. However, this is to be preferred to the wrong way where there is no paññā at all.

Buth Sawong: Some of the listeners would like to ask how the four Applications of Mindfulness should be practised. I have noticed that there is a great deal of wrong practice. Many people practise in the wrong way mindfulness of breath, which is included in the Application of Mindfulness of the Body. They do not know the realities which constitute the body.

Sujin: Please ask questions, because this is a Dhamma discussion. Let us discuss why a person does not practise in the right way.

Buth Sawong: How can people practise in the right way?

Sujin: There is right practice and wrong practice. Now I would like to ask you in my turn: because of what does someone practise in the wrong way?

Buth Sawong: Please can you help us to explain this?

Sujin: The person who asks questions should consider and investigate these questions himself as well. He should find out which cause brings which result. If he does not think over his question himself, he will not know which cause brings which result. It is because of paññā that he can answer himself questions about the practice. If he cannot answer such questions he cannot follow the right practice. You may answer briefly to my question: what is the reason that someone practises in the wrong way?

Buth Sawong: I would like to ask again in a few words: how can someone practise in the right way?

Sujin: Could you just consider the reason why someone does not practise in the right way?

Buth Sawong: Because he does not know the truth.

Sujin: He does not know what is wrong practice. He has ignorance, he does not understand anything. If he would have right understanding he would follow the right practice. Wrong practice is a form of wrong view, micchā-diṭṭhi, and this is conditioned by ignorance. If someone tells other people that sitting is necessary for the right practice, do the people who follow this advice gain any understanding? If they do not gain any understanding while they are sitting, what is the reason for sitting? Understanding is indispensable for the right practice. The Buddha taught the Dhamma with the purpose of helping people to understand the characteristics of realities which are appearing naturally at this moment. The Buddha did not tell people to sit, but he asked them to listen to the Dhamma so that they would gain understanding. If people do not have theoretical understanding of realities which is conditioned by listening, in which way are they practising? If they do not have any understanding there is moha, ignorance, and there is also wrong view which conditions all kinds of wrong practice.

It is essential to understand that there is no self who is practising. Everything is dhamma: right understanding (sammā-diṭṭhi) is dhamma, wrong view (micchā-diṭṭhi) is dhamma, lobha (attachment), alobha (non-attachment), dosa (aversion), adosa (non-aversion), moha, paññā, they all are dhammas, realities which are non-self.

A person who has wrong view will follow the wrong practice, he cannot follow the right practice. Whereas a person who has right understanding cannot follow the wrong practice. If someone tells a person who has right understanding that sitting is necessary for the right practice, he will not sit, because he knows that by just sitting he will not develop any understanding, and that there is thus no reason for him to sit.

Buth Sawong: How should we practice in the right way satipaṭṭhāna, and in particular Mindfulness of Body?

Sujin: Why do you choose any particular object of mindfulness?

Buth Sawong: I read in the scriptures about Mindfulness of Body, but I do not know how to practise it.

Sujin: There are the six doors of the eyes, ears, nose, tongue, bodysense and mind. The objects presenting themselves through these six doors constitute the "world" which appears to us; in fact there are six worlds appearing through the six doors. If there were not those six worlds we would not experience anything. At this moment there is seeing, but one may not know seeing as it is: only a type of reality, a kind of experience, different from thinking or hearing. What appears through the eyes is visible object, and this is different from sound.

The person who realizes the truth at the moment of seeing, hearing, smelling, tasting, experiencing tangible object or thinking, will not have any doubts about the four Applications of Mindfulness: Mindfulness of Body, of Feeling, of Citta and of Dhammas. There may be doubts about the names of the four Applications of Mindfulness, about concepts, but not about realities. The person who realizes the truth knows that there are realities of the body, rūpas, which are appearing time and again. The rūpas appearing all over the body, from head to toes, are dhammas, realities. Citta can experience the reality which appears through the bodysense when the body is touched. Are teeth, blood or heart appearing at this moment?

Buth Sawong: They exist in conventional sense.

Sujin: You can remember that they are there, but do they appear at this moment?

Buth Sawong: They do not appear now.

Sujin: They have already arisen and fallen away. What has already arisen and fallen away does not appear at this moment. But people remember them in a distorted way, as if they would persist. They take the whole body from head to toes for self. That is the wrong remembrance of self (attā saññā).

The Buddha said that all dhammas are non-self, anattā. Rūpa-dhamma is rūpa-dhamma and nāma-dhamma is nāma-dhamma. They have each their own characteristic and nobody can alter these characteristics; they are realities which are non-self. Rūpa-dhamma arises and then falls away very rapidly, but nāma-dhamma which arises falls away even more rapidly then rūpa-dhamma. When the truth has been realized there is nothing left of our life but just one moment of citta which experiences the rūpa or the nāma which is appearing. People cling to the self, they know because of saññā that they have lungs, liver, heart or spleen which seem to persist, but when there is paññā it can realize that this is only thinking. Satipaṭṭhāna is not thinking, it is the development of direct understanding of the characteristics of realities which are appearing.

When we touch any part of the body, the characteristic of softness or hardness appears. Hardness and softness are rūpas which arise and then fall away immediately. Because of saññā we think of different parts of the body and I will give an example of this. Someone who had a leg being amputated still has a feeling that he has that leg. It is saññā, remembrance, which conditions him to think that he still has that leg, although it has been amputated. There is remembrance of all the rūpas of that leg. In reality the rūpa which appears now falls away immediately and, when there are the appropriate conditions, it is replaced by another rūpa which arises and falls away again. However, people think, because of saññā, of their whole body from head to toes, just as in the case of the person who had his leg amputated but still has a feeling that he has that leg. Only when the wrong remembrance of self, attā saññā, because of which one is used to thinking that the whole body exists, has been eradicated, can one really understand that all dhammas are anattā, non-self. Then there is nothing left of the body as a whole, there is only one characteristic of rūpa at a time which is appearing. This is the way to understand the meaning of anattā.

It is difficult to eliminate the wrong remembrance of self. When the rūpa which is cold impinges on a certain part of the body, it falls away immediately, but it is difficult to realize this. There is still remembrance of, "It is I who is sitting", there is still remembrance of arms, legs, head, of the body as a whole. The wrong view of self has not been eradicated. The Buddha explained that, when sati arises and is aware of the characteristic of the reality which is appearing, one at a time, through the bodysense, there is at such a moment the Application of Mindfulness of the Body. The Four Applications of Mindfulness are not something else but mindfulness of what appears through the eyes, the ears, the nose, the tongue, the bodysense or the mind.

People should not select the object of mindfulness, because then there is clinging to an idea of self who can select such an object. Nobody can direct sati to a particular object, it is sati itself which is aware of such or such object. Sati can be aware of what appears through the eyes or of seeing at this moment when there is seeing. At such a moment there is not Mindfulness of Body. There can be Mindfulness of Dhammas or Mindfulness of Citta, depending on conditions. There is no method which tells one to do particular things in order to have Mindfulness of Body, of Feeling, of Citta or of Dhammas. There is no method at all to be followed. The only way to develop satipaṭṭhāna is to gradually understand the realities which are appearing. Sati can be aware of whatever reality is appearing. For example, when there is seeing, there may be awareness of feeling. When there is awareness of the characteristic of feeling, there is at that moment not Mindfulness of Body or Mindfulness of Citta. The Pāli term used in this context is vedanānupassanā[42] satipaṭṭhāna, meaning: consideration or observation of feeling. This shows that paññā develops by being mindful, by considering the characteristics of realities. If people never are aware of the characteristic of feeling, they will continue to take feeling for self.

---

[42] Vedanā means feeling. Anupassanā means viewing, contemplating, consideration.

Chapter 8

The Natural Way to develop Understanding
Dhamma Discussions in Pnompenh (Part Two)

Sujin: There is no particular method which should be followed for the development of satipaṭṭhāna. The understanding acquired by listening which has been accumulated, conditions sati to be aware of the characteristics of realities which are appearing now. Understanding can be developed of the realities which are appearing naturally in daily life. It is of no use to ask which method of practice should be followed. If there is no understanding at this moment, it is necessary to listen to the Dhamma again in order to gain more understanding. In this way people will know at which moment there is sati and at which moment there is no sati but forgetfulness. If someone thinks of practising in the future there is no sati. Realities are appearing already but he does not realize this. It is useless to think of the future which has not come yet. If someone thinks that he will practise in the future he does not know that at this moment there are realities which should be understood. It is not helpful to wonder about what one should do, how one should practise. Sati can be mindful of seeing at the present moment which is real, or of hearing at the present moment which is real. It can be mindful of realities such as softness or hardness which are experienced by touch, of thinking, of happy, unhappy or indifferent feeling, or of pleasant or unpleasant bodily feeling. All these phenomena are real and they can be object of mindfulness.

We do not have to delay the development of understanding, we should not believe that we have to do anything special first. At this moment there is seeing which experiences what appears through the eyesense. There can be mindfulness of seeing. The characteristic of seeing is nāma, an element which experiences an object. We can see, we are different from a dead person who, even though he has eyes, cannot see, who cannot perceive a table or a chair. We can see so long as we are alive and we have not gone blind. At this moment there is seeing and this is only one moment of citta. Nobody can create seeing, it arises because of its appropriate conditions. The citta which is seeing is different from the citta which is hearing. We should remember that these are different realities. Gradually we can come to understand the characteristic of the citta which is seeing at this moment. Understanding cannot yet be clear in the beginning. If someone wonders of what there can be ignorance, the answer is that ignorance does not know as it is seeing which presents itself, that it does not know the true nature of what appears now. Paññā is the opposite of ignorance; paññā understands realities whereas ignorance does not know anything.

Seeing arises because of its appropriate conditions. When sati is aware of seeing, paññā can at that moment understand its nature, it can understand it as a type of reality. Sati and paññā arise and fall away together very rapidly. They arise only when there are conditions for their arising. Nobody can cause their arising, but they can develop little by little. Their development takes a great deal of time. Nobody can, even when sati arises, have clear understanding of realities immediately.

The Buddha, in order to be able to attain Buddhahood, had to fulfil the "perfections" from the time that the Buddha Dīpankara [43] declared him to be a future Buddha, he had to

[43] There were other Buddhas before the Buddha Gotama. The Buddha Gotama was in one of his former lives the brahman Sumedha, aeons ago. In that life he aspired to be a future Buddha.

accumulate them for four incalculable periods and a hundred thousand aeons. Ānanda accumulated the perfections for a hundred thousand aeons. Therefore, why should people ask how they should practise? If someone asks such a question it shows that he wishes to understand immediately the realities which appear at this moment, but this is impossible. The person who develops the eightfold Path must know himself, he must be truthful with regard to himself. At the moment when there is ignorance, he does not understand realities and at the moment when sati arises he can find out that there is awareness. When sati arises it is aware of realities which arise naturally in daily life. At this moment seeing arises naturally in daily life. We can investigate in the right way what seeing is, we can understand that it is a type of reality. At such a moment there is sati arising with theoretical understanding. When there is direct understanding of the characteristic of seeing as nāma, there is satipaṭṭhāna. At such a moment there is understanding of the characteristics of realities as they are, but there cannot be clear, thorough understanding immediately. Understanding has to be developed gradually. The person who develops understanding has no doubt about it that if sati does not arise, if there is no awareness of the characteristics of realities, paññā cannot grow and that thus the characteristics of realities cannot be clearly understood. Therefore, he develops satipaṭṭhāna naturally in his daily life. He realizes that there are moments when sati can be aware of realities, and that there are also moments when sati does not arise, but he has no desire to try to induce the arising of sati. He knows that sati does not arise because of one's desire for it. Each cause brings its appropriate effect. If someone wants to be a person who is intent on kusala he should begin at this moment. If he does not want to be angry he should from now on begin to be less inclined to anger. Kusala dhammas should be developed, they cannot arise just according to our wish. If one wants to develop paññā, one can begin to be aware of the characteristics of realities in a natural way, and there should not be an idea of "I" or self who is aware. When sati arises and it is aware of realities, one can find out that there is sati already and that it is not necessary to make a special effort for sati. Nothing else can be done but gradually developing more understanding of the characteristics of realities.

Someone may feel happy about his understanding or about the arising of sati, but then there is clinging and he should get rid of it. One should not hope for the arising of sati in the future, neither should one cling to sati which has arisen, that is wrong practice. The right practice is the development of awareness of realities just as they appear naturally. When there is right practice, there is no attachment nor aversion with regard to the reality which is appearing, because that reality is not "I", mine or self. Not only in this life there is clinging to the concept of "I" or self, also in countless past lives there was such clinging. How could we then today have immediately clear understanding of the characteristics of nāma and rūpa? If there has not often been listening to the Dhamma and considering it, it is impossible that there is at the moment of awareness of realities direct understanding of their arising and falling away.

When the Buddha taught the Dhamma, there were each time many people who penetrated the four noble Truths, but this does not mean that every listener could attain enlightenment. Those who attained enlightenment to the degree of arahatship were fewer in number than those who attained the third stage of enlightenment, the stage of the non-returner (anāgāmī). Even so, those who became non-returners were fewer in number than those who attained the second stage of enlightenment, the stage of the once-returner (sakadāgāmī), and those who became once-returners were fewer in number than those who attained the first stage of enlightenment, the stage of the streamwinner (sotāpanna). Those who became streamwinners were again fewer in number than those who did not attain any stage of enlightenment. Listening and considering the Dhamma is never enough, people should continue to listen to the Dhamma and consider what they have heard.

When we read the stories about the past lives of the Buddha's disciples, we learn that there were people who, although they studied the whole Tipiṭaka and its commentaries, still did not penetrate the four noble Truths. Therefore, it is of no use to wonder when one will understand the truth. Besides, people should not ask someone else whether they will have right understanding after a long time of development or within a short time. Everybody should know with regard to himself whether at this moment sati is aware of the realities which are appearing, or whether there is no sati. People should know the truth about themselves, and they should be sincere with regard to their own development. The only way which should be followed is to continue developing understanding, little by little.

Buth Sawong: With regard to the practice of the Dhamma, people who have listened to the Dhamma find that realities arise and fall away too rapidly. They say that for this reason they cannot clearly understand them. They still seem to see beings and persons, not visible object, because the different realities arise and fall away too rapidly. They feel that they are not fast enough to discern different realities.

Sujin: Are they not fast enough to understand realities, or do they not understand them at all ?

Buth Sawong: They know them as beings, people and self.

Sujin: Is this a matter of being too slow to understand realities, or of just not understanding them at all?

Buth Sawong: Actually, they do not understand realities, and this is not a matter of being too slow to catch them.

Sujin: That is right. At this moment realities are appearing to all of us, because we are not asleep[44]. There is seeing, but is there understanding which knows that seeing is a reality which experiences something, that there is no "I" who is seeing? That which is experienced through the eyes, visible object, is appearing. Is there understanding of it already? We should not look for that which appears through the eyes, it is there already. At this moment realities are appearing, but they are not known as they are. This, however, is not a matter of being too slow to catch them. Therefore, people should not say that they are too slow to understand dhammas; they have only theoretical understanding of the fact that realities arise and fall away very rapidly. At this moment realities are arising and falling away and it is of no use to think that one is too slow to realize this. Only paññā which has been developed can realize the truth of impermanence. What has fallen away has fallen away, nobody can alter this fact. During the time when someone is thinking that he is too slow to realize the falling away of realities, realities still arise again and fall away again. The only way which can be followed is developing understanding of the characteristic of what appears at this very moment, and this does not have to be delayed. This is the way to check one's own understanding, to find out whether there is understanding of the true nature of realities or not yet. If someone gradually has more understanding of realities, it means that paññā is developing.

Does one want to attain enlightenment without knowing as they are the characteristics of realities appearing at this moment? That is impossible. So long as someone has not penetrated the truth of the realities appearing now he should not believe that he will realize the four noble Truths, that

---

[44] When we are fast asleep and not dreaming, there are bhavanga-cittas or life-continuum. These cittas do not arise within processes of cittas which experience objects through the six doors.

he will attain nibbāna. Everybody can repeat the Dhamma
he has heard, he can repeat that realities arise because of
conditions, and that the realities which have arisen can be
experienced. However, when at this moment something hard
is touched, do people have direct understanding of the truth,
namely, that hardness which is experienced by touch appears
because it has arisen, and that if hardness does not arise it
cannot be experienced by touch? Everybody is touching one
thing or other and if sati does not arise people think that it
is a table or a hand which is experienced by touch. When
sati arises it can be aware of the characteristic of hardness,
but this does not mean that paññā is able to penetrate the
true nature of realities immediately. We should remember
the Buddha's words we read in the scriptures, about being
mindful often, again and again[45]. Only if there is mindfulness
again and again will it be understood that hardness is a
kind of rūpa, different from the reality which experiences
hardness, from nāma. When there has been mindfulness
more often of the characteristics of nāma and rūpa, paññā
can become keener and reach the degree of insight-
knowledge, vipassanā ñāṇa, and at that moment realities
appear as they are. This does not mean, however, that the
arising and falling away of realities can be penetrated
immediately. In the course of the development of paññā
there are different stages of insight-knowledge, and the
arising and falling away of realities is not penetrated at the
first stage of insight-knowledge, but at a later stage[46]. When
someone believes that he can immediately penetrate the
arising and falling away of realities he is on the wrong way.

---

[45] See for example the Satpaṭṭhāna Sutta, Middle Length Saings I, 10,
where it is said after each section of Mindfulness of the Body, "Thus he
lives contemplating the body in the body...", and after the other sections,
that he lives contemplating feelings in the feelings, citta in citta,
dhammas in dhammas.

[46] At the first stage the difference between the characteristic of nāma
and the characteristic of rūpa is clearly distinguished.

He should not think of having to be in time to "catch" the arising and falling away of realities. He should begin to understand the characteristic of the reality which experiences something, of nāma, and of the characteristic of the reality which does not experience anything, of rūpa. He can begin to be aware of the realities appearing through the eyes, ears, nose, tongue, bodysense and mind. There are only six doorways through which realities are appearing, but ignorance cannot understand this.

The Buddha taught the Dhamma in detail for fortyfive years, he taught the Vinaya (Book of Discipline for the monks), the Suttanta (Discourses) and the Abhidhamma. He taught the Dhamma in so many details, because he knew the amount of our ignorance. Realities are only nāma and rūpa, but the Buddha taught different aspects of them: he taught the four Applications of Mindfulness so that we would be able to understand realities as non-self. He taught, for example, the Application of Mindfulness of Feeling, so that we would know the truth that the different feelings, including happy feeling, unhappy feeling, indifferent feeling, pleasant and painful bodily feeling, are not "I", not self. We can notice today that there are many kinds of nāma and rūpa, realities appearing through the eyes, ears, nose, tongue, bodysense and mind. Feeling arises each time when there is seeing, hearing, smelling, tasting, experiencing tangible object or thinking.

When we take into account the reality of feeling, we see that it is manifold, but apart from feeling there are also, for example, lobha (attachment), dosa (aversion), jealousy, avarice and many other kinds of akusala cetasikas. Besides these there are also many kinds of sobhana (beautiful) cetasikas. All these realities which arise time and again are dependant on the appropriate conditions. In our daily life there is forgetfulness and ignorance when there is no awareness of the characteristics of realities which are appearing.

Buth Sawong: I received a question from someone who asked what a person who practises satipaṭṭhāna should do when he is near death.

Sujin: There is no "I", no self who can do anything. There are only citta, cetasika and rūpa which arise time and again because of their appropriate conditions.

Buth Sawong: When at death rūpa has fallen away, nāma also has fallen away. What is it that will be reborn?

Sujin: There will again be the arising of nāma and rūpa. Is it not true that just a moment ago nāma and rūpa fell away?

Buth Sawong: That is true.

Sujin: Is there again arising of nāma and rūpa?

Buth Sawong: Yes.

Sujin: Nāma and rūpa arise and then fall away completely according to conditions, all the time. If nāma and rūpa would not arise we would not be sitting here.

Buth Sawong: When I and my relatives came to meet you at the airport, you said about us that we have paññā. Paññā in what respect?

Sujin: Did your relatives who came to meet me not listen to the Dhamma you explained in your lectures?

Buth Sawong: They did.

Sujin: If they had not gained understanding from listening, would they listen again?

Buth Sawong: They have listened and gained understanding from what they heard.

Sujin: That is paññā which understands.

Glossary

Abhidhammattha Sangaha an Encyclopedia of the Abhidhamma, written by Anuruddha between the 8th and the 12th century A.D.

Ācariya The Pāli term for teacher

adosa non aversion

ājīva livelihood

akusala unwholesome, unskilful

alobha non attachment, generosity

amoha wisdom or understanding

anāgāmī non returner, person who has reached the third stage of enlightenment, he has no aversion (dosa)

Ānanda the chief attendant of the Buddha

anantara paccaya contiguity condition

anattā not self

anumodhanā thanksgiving, appreciation of someone else's kusala

arahat noble person who has attained the fourth and last stage of enlightenment

ariyan noble person who has attained enlightenment

attā self

avijjā ignorance

āyatanas sense-fields, namely the five senses and the mind and the objects experienced by them

bhāvanā mental development, comprising the development of calm and the development of insight

bhavanga-citta life-continuum

bodhisatta a being destined to become a Buddha

Buddha a fully enlightened person who has discovered the truth all by himself, without the aid of a teacher

cetasika mental factor arising with consciousness

citta consciousness, the reality which knows or cognizes an object

dāna generosity, giving

dhamma reality, truth, the teachings

dhātu element

diṭṭhi wrong view, distorted view of realities

dosa aversion or ill will

dukkha suffering, unsatisfactoriness of conditioned realities

ekaggatā concentration, one-pointedness, a cetasika which has the function to focus on one object

ganthas bonds, a group of defilements

indriya faculty. Some are rūpas such as the sense organs, some are nāmas such as feeling. Five 'spiritual faculties' are wholesome faculties which should be cultivated, namely: confidence, energy, awareness, concentration and wisdom.

kamma intention or volition; deed motivated by volition

kammajā-rūpa rūpa which is originated by kamma

kāya body. It can also stand for the 'mental body', the cetasikas

khandhas aggregates of conditioned realities classified as five groups: physical phenomena, feelings, perception or remembrance, activities or formations (cetasikas other than feeling or perception), consciousness.

khaṇika maraṇa momentary death of a reality

kusala wholesome, skilful

lobha attachment, greed

lokuttara citta supramundane citta which experiences nibbāna

magga path (eightfold Path)

mettā loving kindness

micchā-samādhi wrong concentration

moha ignorance

moha-mūla-citta citta rooted in ignorance

nāma mental phenomena,including those which are conditioned and also the unconditioned nāma which is nibbāna.

ñāṇa wisdom, insight

nibbāna unconditioned reality, the reality which does not arise and fall away. The destruction of lust, hatred and delusion. The deathless. The end of suffering.

paccaya condition

Pāli the language of the Buddhist teachings

paññā wisdom or understanding

paramattha dhamma truth in the absolute sense: mental and physical phenomena, each with their own characteristic.

rūpa physical phenomena, realities which do not experience anything

sacca truth

saddhā confidence

sakadāgāmī once-returner, a noble person who has attained the second stage of enlightenment

samādhi concentration or one-pointedness, ekaggatā cetasika

samatha the development of calm

sammā right

Sangha community of monks and nuns. As one of the triple Gems it means the community of those people who have attained enlightenment.

saññā memory, remembrance or "perception"

saṅkāra dhamma conditioned dhamma

sati awareness, non-forgetfulness, awareness of reality by direct experience

satipaṭṭhāna applicatioms of mindfulness. It can mean the cetasika sati which is aware of realities or the objects of mindfulness which are classified as four applications of mindfulness: Body, Feeling Citta, Dhamma. Or it can mean the development of direct understanding of realities through awareness.

sīla morality in action or speech, virtue

sīlabbata-parāmāsā wrong practice

sobhana (citta and cetasika) beautiful, accompanied by beautiful roots

sota-viññāṇa hearing-consciousness

sotāpanna person who has attained the first stage of enlightenment, and who has eradicated wrong view of realities

sukha happy, pleasant

sutta part of the scriptures containing dialogues at different places on different occasions.

suttanta a sutta text

Tipiṭaka the teachings of the Buddha

upekkhā indifferent feeling. It can stand for evenmindedness or equanimity and then it is not feeling

vācī speech

vedanā feeling

vedanānupassanā satipaṭṭhāna mindfulness of feeling

vinaya Book of Discipline for the monks

viññāṇa consciousness, citta

vipākacitta citta which is the result of a wholesome deed (kusala kamma) or an unwholesome deed (akusala kamma). It can arise as rebirth-consciousness, or during life as the experience of pleasant or unpleasant objects through the senses, such as seeing, hearing, etc.

vipassanā wisdom which sees realities as they are

Visuddhimagga an encyclopaedia of the Buddha's teaching, written by Buddhaghosa in the fifth century A.D

vitakka applied thinking

Buddhist Phrases

*From discussions with Sujin Boriharnwanaket
and Phra Dhammadhara*

If one does not realise yet that one has wrong understanding,
it is impossible to develop right understanding.

The beginning is understanding the characteristic of
awareness correctly.

Some people are afraid to watch TV, but now we are lost in
the concepts with no awareness.

One takes subtle attachment for calmness because of lack
of understanding of calmness.

Life is so short, so fragile. Get rid of attachment.

Always burning with lobha, dosa, moha ...renunciation
with satipatthana...

Understand accumulations from moment to moment.

Right action is abstaining from wrong action. There must
be awareness of a nāma or rūpa to be right action of the
eightfold path.

The aim of thinking about concepts in the right way is to
know more about realities.

Seeing sees visible object. What is seen is not a person. We
have attachment to individuals, but individuality has no
separate characteristic.

If you think you are so clever and others don't think so, you feel sorry. Attachment to self brings sorrow.

Aversion prevents listening.

The understanding that begins to know conditioned realities is also conditioned.

The arising of any conditioned reality is dukkha because of its arising. If there is no arising, there is no dukkha. If there is no awareness of the reality now, how can one understand the absolute reality of dukkha?

The arising happens because there is passing away of previous moments. Once there is no arising there can be total peace and calm.

Can you tell what is beyond this moment?

If there is no thinking of this or that concept, can there be concept at this moment?

The game of life that tanha always wins.

Don't be a victim of the conceptual system, but the conqueror of your ignorance.

When there is dosa, there is strong lobha somewhere that has conditioned it.

Propagating wrong view is the most dangerous thing to do.

Don't force yourself to think it is the right time and right place for the arising of awareness, because awareness can arise anytime or place. Don't limit it.

At the moment of developing right understanding, there is real rest no matter what one is doing.
Without satipaṭṭhāna, there is always cling to self, always wanting the best for self, even wanting more understanding.

We think it's enough listening so now we need time and place for the development, but in reality it's never enough listening.

We don't understand the game of taṇhā (craving), so we follow it wherever it goes.

The Buddha taught us to listen to dhamma, not people.

Let go of desire and attachment for other objects that do not appear now. When there's awareness, there's letting go.

The Buddha taught everyone to have kusala citta at any moment, at any level, because to have kusala citta at any moment is so helpful.

Right understanding brings detachment. If there is even a little attachment, it hinders the progress of right understanding.

Samatha doesn't get rid of concepts.

As understanding grows, it grows beyond the level of thinking of sammuti sacca and knows the difference between paramattha sacca and sammuti sacca (concept) instead of clinging to sammuti sacca and taking for self.

We must be brave enough to study with panna any reality. We need to be brave to begin to study visible object as visible object.

It is kindness to others if we don't cling to them or encourage them to be attached to us.

The test is at this moment. Test now...Visual object now is the test of whether one has understanding or whether there should be more understanding developed.

With understanding and awareness of calmness, calmness grows.

The world of paramattha sacca is the world of understanding reality as it is.

One is burnt by one's desire all the time. In reality one is attached to one's feeling, not really the person...

Attachment is only a conditioned moment. Attachment is like a trap or a bait.

One kills oneself and one's heart by one's attachment and ignorance. We are trapped, lured by attachment all the time. It's truly poisonous.

We are cut up with sammuti sacca when there is no awareness of thinking.

There are different conditions for different namas and rupas. With more understanding of different conditions you will see that there is no self.

It needs right understanding to know whether this moment is kusala or akusala.

Other Publications

The Buddha's Path
By Nina van Gorkom

Explains the basic principles of Buddhism to those who
have no previous experience and knowledge of this way of
life. The four noble Truths - suffering - the origin of
suffering - the cessation of suffering - and the way leading
to the end of suffering - are explained as a philosophy and a
practical guidance which can be followed in today's world.
The contents include: the Buddha's life, the truth of
suffering, the truth of non-self, the mind, deeds and their
results, good deeds and a wholesome life, meditation and
the Eightfold Path. 1994, paperback, 150 pages, 140mm x
210mm, ISBN 1 897633 12 2, price £7.95.

Buddhism in Daily Life
By Nina van Gorkom
A general introduction to the main ideas of Theravāda
Buddhism. The purpose of this book is to help the reader
gain insight into the Buddhist scriptures and the way in
which the teachings can be used to benefit both ourselves
and others in everyday life. Several chapters are written in
the form of question and answer, inspired by questions
posed by ordinary people who were confronted with
difficulties in the practical application of the teachings. The
book will be an invaluable aid for those individuals who
wish to develop the Buddhist path to true understanding.
Suitable for both practising Buddhists and newcomers to
the teachings. ISBN 1 897633 16 5, 192 pages, paperback,
135mm x 210mm, price £7.95

Mettā: loving kindness in Buddhism
By Sujin Boriharnwanaket
An introduction to the basic Buddhist teachings of metta,
loving kindness, and its practical application in today's
world. It shows metta as the "foundation of the world"
essential for peace and happiness of both ourselves and
others. It gives guidance to its development, explaining
conditions for it and impediments to it. And shows the
importance of the Buddhist meditation practice of insight
for its development. 1995
ISBN 1 897633 14 9, 128 pages, paperback, 210mm x
135mm, price £7.95.

The World in the Buddhist Sense
By Nina van Gorkom
Explains the realities in and around ourselves. Analyses the difference between the development of calm and the development of insight. Discusses the meditation practice of "mindfulness of breathing". Illustrates with many quotes from the Pāli Tipiṭaka. Suitable for those who have a background of Buddhism but who seek a deeper understanding. October 1993, 123 pp, paperback, 210mm x 140mm. ISBN 1 897633 11 4, price £7.95.

Abhidhamma in Daily Life
By Nina van Gorkom
We live mostly in a changing world of ideas. We are caught up in concepts. What is real and important can be lost as we strive to compete. Abhidhamma in Daily Life goes straight to the heart of Buddhist doctrine. It defines what is real with the aim of freeing us from the daily rat race.

The purpose of the book is to give a fundamental understanding of the five senses: seeing, hearing, touching, tasting, smelling and the all important sixth sense, the mind. Only when we truly understand these six senses can we begin to comprehend what is important and truly real.

Abhidhamma in Daily Life shows us how to apply the basic precepts of Buddhist teaching in our daily life which will impact not only on ourselves, but also on those around us. It cuts through the complexities of the original text, the Pāli Tipiṭaka, simplifying the scriptures without losing their meaning. Many Pāli terms are used, but they are defined as they are introduced making it suitable for the beginner as well as practising Buddhists.

Abhidhamma in Daily Life is a vital key for unlocking the deep meaning of the Buddha's teachings and the Buddhist way of life.
ISBN 1 897633 17 3, 272 pages, paperback, 135mm x 216mm, price £11.95, US $17.95.

Cetasikas
by Nina van Gorkom

Cetasika means 'belonging to the mind'. It is a mental factor
which accompanies consciousness (citta) and experiences
an object. There are 52 cetasikas. This book gives an outline
of each of these 52 cetasikas and shows the relationship
they have with each other. It will help the student have
more understanding of the intricate operations of the mind
enabling the development of good qualities and the
eventual eradication of all defilements. It will help to
understand that citta and cetasika act according to their
own conditions and that an abiding agent (soul or self) is
not to be found. The book assumes some previous knowlege
of Buddhism.

First edition, author: Nina van Gorkom, ISBN 1897633 18
1, 416 pages, 216mm x 135mm, hardback,
price £24, Publication date 1st April 1999.